# COMPANION TO THE DIRECTORY FOR CATECHESIS

Petroc Willey and Joseph D. White

*All books are published
thanks to the generosity of the supporters
of the Catholic Truth Society*

Dedication
*For Katherine and Ana*

## About the Authors

**Petroc Willey** is blessed to be married to Katherine and has four children – Charis, Benedict, Nicholas and David, and four grandchildren. Originally from England, he now lives in Steubenville, Ohio, where he is a Professor of Theology and Director of the Catechetical Institute at Franciscan University. Petroc has worked in Catholic education and formation, in Oxford and Birmingham, and now in the United States, for more than thirty-five years, in university, seminary and lay institutions, and in both traditional and distance education. He was appointed by Pope Benedict XVI as a Consultor for the Pontifical Council for the Promotion of the New Evangelization.

**Joseph D. White** converted to the Catholic faith while in graduate school at Virginia Commonwealth University, where he received a PhD. in Clinical Psychology. He later studied Catholic Theology at St Mary's University in San Antonio. Joseph White served as a parish Director of Faith Formation for two years, and then served for seven years as Director of Family Counseling and Family Life for the Diocese of Austin, Texas. He now works as Director of Catechetical Resources for OSV Publishing and Curriculum and teaches courses in Catechetical Ministry at Holy Apostles College and Seminary. Joseph White has written thirteen books and numerous articles about catechesis, Catholic education, spirituality, and ministry. He lives with his wife, Ana, in Texas.

Published 2021 by The Incorporated Catholic Truth Society
42-46 Harleyford Road London SE11 5AY
Tel: 020 7640 0042
© 2021 The Incorporated Catholic Truth Society.
www.ctsbooks.org

ISBN 978 1 78469 655 9

# Contents

# Foreword

by Most Rev. Dr. Franz-Peter Tebartz-van Elst

*Delegate for Catechesis at the Pontifical Council*
*for the Promotion of the New Evangelisation*

The edition of the new *Directory for Catechesis* is a milestone in the catechetical development of the Catholic Church. The first edition of 1971 took over the Second Vatican Council's inspiration for the transmission of the faith. The second edition of 1997 gathered the numerous advances in the catechetical field and incorporated the *Catechism of the Catholic Church* promulgated five years before in 1992. This second directory of 1997 became, more so than the first, an essential text on catechesis for the Universal Church and its framework marked the scope of a fundamental catechesis. The shaping of all catechetical endeavors according to the paradigm of the early Church's catechumenal process initiated a revival in catechumenal thinking and practice. Subsequently, local churches made appropriate adaptations needed by their varying situations. For more than twenty years, this second directory had been a guiding text until gradually it became clear, given all the cultural changes, that an update was necessary.

About five years ago, the Pontifical Council for the Promotion of the New Evangelisation was charged with making the said revision; however, the conditions for transmitting the faith in modern societies had been changing so rapidly since 1997 that a simple revision became inadequate. After spending much time and energy working with experts from all over the world and in close collaboration with bishops, who are the primary catechists of their local churches (ref. CD/2020, n. 114), a new directory was produced. On 25th June 2020, this new *Directory for Catechesis*, previously approved for publication by Pope Francis, was presented to the Universal Church. The new directory fully embraced the Holy Father's Apostolic Exhortation, *Evangelii Gaudium*, and its call for the urgent intensification of the transmission of the faith or evangelisation.

His Excellency Archbishop Rino Fisichella, the President of the Pontifical Council for the Promotion of the New Evangelisation, has highlighted the changing culture and part of the needs that led to a new directory in these words: *"Today the Church is facing a great challenge in the form of digital culture. Focusing on a phenomenon that imposes itself as global requires that those who are responsible for the formation do not prevaricate. In contrast with the past, when culture was limited to the geographical context, digital culture is entwined with the ongoing globalisation and even determines its development."*[1] Evangelisation and catechesis under these conditions reflect the call of the Second Vatican Council to bring the Gospel to where people live and act, in short, to their daily globalised world. This effort requires a constant reflection on the meaning and purpose of catechesis as it responds to the "signs of the times".

Three months after its publication, this Pontifical Council has already received encouraging reactions and reflections from all corners of the universal Church. This *Companion to the Directory for Catechesis* by Doctors Petroc Willey and Joseph White is one such response. This publication is an example of how this new *Directory* can be introduced not only to institutions but also and most importantly to catechists and interested persons. This *Companion* follows closely the structure and layout of the new *Directory*, itself founded on five major aspects to be outlined subsequently.

## I   THE OPTION OF MERCY

The episcopal and papal motto of Pope Francis, *"miserando atque eligendo"* is a clear indication of what catechesis is all about. Willey and White capture this sense in explaining the first chapter of the new directory and its fundamental theological significance. In contrast to the previous directories for catechesis, this *new* directory mentions the concept of mercy about twenty-five times (ref. 1971: 4 times; 1997: 4 times). By the sheer number of references to mercy it can be perceived that the new directory seeks to highlight the spirituality of mercy with its reference to thinking and acting in merciful ways based on the way Jesus himself has revealed the Eternal Father, "who is rich in mercy". How Jesus showed sympathy, compassion, and

---

[1] *Conferenza Stampa di presentazione del Direttorio per la Catechesi redatto dal Pontificio Consiglio per la Promozione della Nuova Evangelizzazione*, 25th June 2020. Source: *http://press.vatican.va/content/salastampa/it/bollettino/pubblico/2020/06/25/0356/00812.html.*

empathy to humankind characterises and profiles a catechesis of mercy. The authors of this *Companion* touch upon this aspect of the *Directory* and speak of how disciples need to be formed into a "people of mercy" (p. 35). This *Companion* helps the reader understand what the new directory means by catechesis and it builds bridges between the content of the faith and the daily situations and challenges of life.

This *Companion* also helps us understand how much catechesis is part of the Lord's mandate to evangelise. Catechesis explains the content of the faith and responds to the fundamental questions of life. Catechesis is performed within a cultural context and responds to cultural exigencies yet, as the authors of this *Companion* highlight, referencing the new directory, the doctrine of faith not only transcends culture but can also "reinvigorate every culture" (p. 35). Willey and White, commenting on the identity of catechesis outlined in the second chapter of the new directory, give insights on how the central message of our faith is revealed in Jesus Christ, on his filiation, on his relationship to the Eternal Father and on his self-communication. Catechesis is Christ-centred and an authentic catechesis will always lead us to a personal encounter and communion with Jesus Christ, the mercy of the Father made human, like us.

## II   THE SCOPE OF MISSION

This *Companion to the Directory for Catechesis* aligns itself with Pope Francis's *Evangelii Gaudium*, the "magna carta" of the new evangelisation and the call to mission that needs to be embraced by all Catholics. Chapters three and four of this *Companion* contain a very inspiring view on catechists, their ministry and the requirement for a permanent formation in the mission of the Church. The authors of this *Companion* comment on catechists' identity and formation by referencing important Church documents and previous pontifical teachings on this matter. This fact conveys a strong sense of tradition and allows for an understanding that is part of the greater framework of revelation as found in Holy Scripture and the teaching of the Magisterium.

The new directory is fully aware of the need for the Church's mission to be fully cognisant of what has changed in our world, in our cultures and in modern societies. This *Companion* helps us comprehend how and where this knowledge of a changing world has to be reflected in different catechetical ministries and in the formation of catechists. Creating a missionary identity that proposes the contents of the faith in an authentic way is a challenge. A missionary catechesis not only needs to relate Church doctrine to the current problems and issues of concrete persons but it also needs to communicate the faith effectively. Catechists have to learn, in new ways, this missionary identity since the supporting structures for the transmission of the faith are becoming weaker and weaker. A mission-oriented scope is spirituality rooted in *1 Peter* 3:15 that says, *"Always be ready to make your defense to anyone who demands from you an accounting for the hope that is in you".* All disciples and catechists are called to offer this defense with their words and actions and even with their lives.

Petroc Willey and Joseph White also highlight the role of the catechist as someone who "accompanies", as noted in the new directory. Accompaniment is not entering a journey of "endless wandering" without a destination. It is rather a "journeying" and "staying with the person on that journey" on that mission that leads to Christ. It is "travelling *together*" on that journey (p. 59, italics added). Catechists accompany others with humble patience, without a superiority that creates distance, and they are always in formation, because they are certain that they do not know it all. Those who are looking for faith find in their own catechists examples of how faith provides deeper human insights particularly in times of crisis, and how Jesus Christ will never abandon them on their road to holiness.

## III  THE MEANING OF *"KERYGMA"*

As already noted in *Evangelii Gaudium,* the *"kerygma"* as it applies to catechesis, or *kerygmatic catechesis*, has become a central theme in the new *Directory for Catechesis* (ref. *DC*, n. 57ff.). *Kerygmatic* catechesis announces or proclaims the core of the Christian faith. This Gospel message of salvation is transmitted through a *first proclamation* that touches the hearts of not only baptised believers but also of people who are searching for the ultimate truth and meaning in their lives. In paragraph fifty-four, the new directory describes the *kerygma* as "the fire of the Spirit" that is given to persons in "a form of a tongue" moving them to "believe in Jesus Christ that with his death and resurrection communicates the Father's infinite mercy" (ref. *DC*, n.54). *Kerygma* in catechesis can be understood as a catechesis that never abandons the *first announcement*, the most basic, "the elementals", and brings the central aspects of the faith to very specific life situations moving believers and non-believers to conversion.

This dynamic process of the proclamation of the faith is not a theory. The *first announcement* in catechesis also includes the *"via pulchritudinis"* (ref. *Evangelii Gaudium*, n. 167), that *way of beauty* is particularly found in the liturgy for it is a way that brings us closer to Christ. The *first announcement* is a necessary part of the catechumenal process that bring persons to the thresholds of faith and later on fortifies their faith. The Church has already discovered, outlined, and internalised the catechumenate. Willey and White highlight these aspects in this *Companion* book. They help the reader understand what the new directory is saying about the importance of the *mystagogical* process in the transmission of the faith.

The *kerygma* or the announcement of what God has revealed (the *"fides quae"*) elicits a personal response or abandonment to God (the *"fides qua"*). The act of faith entails both dimensions (ref. *DC*, n. 18). People open themselves up to a personal encounter with the love of God made concrete, palpable in the Lord Jesus Christ by listening to the Word of God proclaimed in the Holy Scriptures. Persons respond by entrusting themselves and giving the deep consent of their hearts to the Lord Jesus, doing thus, many times through spontaneous prayers of thanksgiving and praise. Faith is received and accepted but it also leads believers to express it in concrete acts of charity. *Kerygmatic* catechesis in the new directory follows and develops that which was previously outlined in *Evangelii Gaudium* (ref. *EG*, n. 163-175) and therefore recommends that every communication of the faith and its learning be inspired by it and by the catechumenal process of which it is an integral part (ref. *DC*, n. 61ff).

## IV  THE EVALUATION OF DIGITAL CULTURE

In the press conference introducing the new directory, His Excellency Archbishop Fisichella, referring to the challenge of the digital culture, stated: "The instruments created in this last decade manifest a radical transformation of behaviours that influence above all *the formation of personal identity and interpersonal relations.*"[2] The Church operates within and through this digital culture and the complex human relationships it entails. Catechesis, therefore, must respond to this reality.

In this *Companion* Petroc Willey and Joseph White provide accurate comments on the significance of digital culture in today's world and its challenges and limits for the transmission of the faith. Referencing the *Directory*'s chapter seven on Methodology in Catechesis, these authors state, "*The* Directory *emphasises the importance of reaching people in the modern world with tools they are accustomed to using in other learning environments. In addition, we are warned about the profound impact the digital world can*

---

[2]  *Conferenza Stampa di presentazione del Direttorio per la Catechesi redatto dal Pontificio Consiglio per la Promozione della Nuova Evangelizzazione*, 25th June 2020. Source: *http://press.vatican.va/content/ salastampa/it/bollettino/pubblico/2020/06/25/0356/00812.html.* Italics added.

*make, especially on younger generations, with regard to identity and emotional regulation, and cautioned that the virtual world cannot replace real life interactions, especially in our Catholic faith"* (p. 118).

All reflections on digital communication, its opportunities and challenges, are embedded in the larger context about the general importance of language, community, and space in catechesis. This widened vision helps us realise that catechetical communication is more than just the simple exchange of information. In this regard, one also needs to recognise the way Catholics understand and practise liturgy and the catechetical implications of the liturgical language itself. Personal participation in the liturgy can never be substituted by an online participation. It is apparent that digital support in catechesis cannot replace mystagogical ways of sharing the faith and of deepening one's spirituality. Willey and White, to their merit, respond to these concerns in this *Companion*.

## V  THE PROCESS OF LEARNING

Pope St John Paul II in *Catechesi Tradendae* (ref. *CT*, art. 35-45) already underlined that all stages and ages in life require catechesis and that faith learning is a lifelong process. This important understanding can be found under various aspects in the new *Directory for Catechesis*. Chapter eight details the catechetical road to follow in relation to different ages and groups and the need to consider and respond to the specific concerns of their stage in life. The new directory also focuses on catechesis with specific populations including migrants, disabled persons, prisoners, and those in extreme poverty. Chapters nine and ten discuss ecclesial contexts and their responsibilities. The digital world is once again considered, as is the importance of facing its prospects and limits in catechesis (ref. *DC*, n. 370ff). Chapter eleven discusses the *inculturation* of the faith and the last chapter presents a general orientation and overview directed at the hierarchical levels in the Church that need to accept, respond to, and be guided by this new *Directory for Catechesis*.

Petroc Willey and Joseph White enrich their *Companion* to the new directory by explicitly stating that all these aspects belong to a *holistic* process of faith learning. Their way of following the chapters of the new directory is not just a repetition or even a paraphrase of their content but a method by which the relevance of the *Directory's* content is made manifest under different conditions. This *Companion* provides a detailed explanation of what the new directory is about and is a welcomed contribution and support for catechists who will benefit greatly in their ministry with this guided reflection.

## CONCLUSION

This *Companion to the Directory for Catechesis* by Doctors Petroc Willey and Joseph White is a valuable addition to the many responses that the *Directory* has elicited and is an indication of what that the Franciscan University of Steubenville stands for with its focus on catechesis, spiritual formation and unity with the Chair of Peter. This *Companion* also includes at the end of each chapter, and worthy to be mentioned, a prayer for catechists and questions for reflection. Both authors are to be commended in their effort with this book to further the new evangelisation and its catechetical dimension in our times.

*From the Vatican, Feast of the Nativity of the Blessed Virgin Mary, 8th September 2020.*

✠ Most Rev. Dr. Franz-Peter Tebartz-van Elst

*Delegate for Catechesis at the Pontifical Council*
*for the Promotion of the New Evangelisation*

# Introduction

"When catechesis is done well", St John Paul II wrote, "everything else is easier to do".[3] *Everything* else. Catechesis is the handing on of the Church's saving doctrine. Everything else in the pastoral life of the Church and in the individual lives of Christians flows more easily when catechesis is undertaken according to the Church's vision and following her guidance. And it is the role of a *Directory for Catechesis* to expound that vision and provide that guidance, precisely and wisely, and in an accessible way, for a new generation.

The publication of a new *Directory for Catechesis*, then, is an event of extraordinary importance for the Church. Catechesis, undertaken well, is the communication of the Father's loving and salvific plan to all the baptised, together with counsel for how to co-operate with the Holy Spirit in making a wholehearted response to that plan of goodness. Catechesis anchors us in the central truths we need to know and understand in order to live the Christian life. It is therefore central to the Church's pastoral ministry – all of the ways in which the Church nourishes and strengthens faith, hope and love in the Christian community for the sake of growth towards maturity in the Body until at last the "whole Christ"[4] is formed, "a people which acknowledges him in truth

---

[3] St John Paul II, *Catechesi Tradendae*, (16th October 1979): 63.
[4] The whole Christ – that is, the *Christus totus* of Christ together with the members of his Body (cf. *Catechism of the Catholic Church* 795).

and serves him in holiness".[5] If we can say that the overall purpose of the Church's pastoral work is that of shepherding God's people into everlasting life, guarding them from harm and guiding them to heaven, then catechesis is the annunciation and presentation of the secure pathways to be followed towards this destination.

When catechesis is done well, everything else is easier to do. Conversely, when catechesis is done badly, or not at all, everything else is *harder* to do. If the Church lacks a vibrant catechesis, the baptised lack direction, cannot easily attain an understanding of the shape and grandeur of the faith, suffer from confusion about how to live in Christ, and are vulnerable to incomplete and fragmentary views of the faith; initial conversion is not consolidated and strengthened, faith lacks any mature integration with life, and the sacraments are experienced as isolated, strange events in a world that is not yet seen with "Catholic eyes".

Catechesis stands at the very heart of the Church's mission and there is an urgency to the carrying out of this mission which is expressed in the phrase "new evangelisation". This new *Directory* has been written, for the first time, by the body in the Holy See that is responsible for supporting the Church in undertaking a renewed evangelisation and catechesis of all of the baptised, the Pontifical Council for the Promotion of the New Evangelisation. It is no accident that the overall responsibility for catechesis has been placed within a body concerned with the overarching mission of evangelisation. The integration of catechesis with evangelisation is a major theme in the *Directory*. The "newness" of the new evangelisation is not an invitation for innovation in the faith or for the kind of "updating" that merely outdates the "old", or for experimentation for the sake of a supposed "relevance" that would render the Christian message shortly irrelevant. The newness of the new evangelisation is that of the Gospel which is "ever ancient, ever new"[6] and of Christ, the One who is the same yesterday, today and forever and who, when he encounters us, makes all things new in our lives and in our cultures.[7] Catechesis is ultimately *his* work. It is *he* who teaches and forms us in his Church, as members of his Body. On page after page the *Directory* makes that truth clear to the reader.

In this *Companion* we have written a text that we hope will set the *Directory* in its present-day context, highlighting its central themes, explaining key terms and unpacking implications for our catechetical ministry. We do not intend this to be read instead of the *Directory*, but hope that it makes that document accessible to all. Petroc Willey is largely responsible for the commentary on the first six chapters and Joseph White for the commentary on chapters seven to twelve.

---

[5] Second Vatican Council, Dogmatic Constitution on the Church, *Lumen Gentium* (21st November 1964): 9.
[6] St Augustine described God, as beauty "ever ancient, ever new" (*Confessions* 10, 26).
[7] Cf. *Hebrews* 13:8; *Revelation* 21:5.

We owe countless debts of gratitude to colleagues, both in the academy and in the field, for their catechetical friendship, their faithfulness to the Church's Magisterium on catechesis and for their generously shared insights over the years into the craft of catechesis. We are also deeply grateful to Bishop Franz-Peter Tebartz-van Elst for his kindness in writing the Foreword to this *Companion* and to Scott Richert at Our Sunday Visitor and Piero Finaldi and Victoria Seed at the Catholic Truth Society for their enthusiastic support and assistance.

Petroc Willey
Joseph D. White

*The Nativity of the Blessed Virgin Mary, 8th September 2020.*

# The *Directory's* Preface and Introduction

The Preface and Introduction to this work provide us with an overview of the document, acting like a grand overture to an opera, setting out the main themes that will be heard throughout the whole work and preparing the reader to be especially attentive to elements of particular importance.

## CHRIST AT THE CENTRE

The Preface reminds us that all that is written in this *Directory* is at the service of making *God's saving work in Christ known and loved*. Everything in the *Directory* has been written in order to "make more evident the goal of catechesis, which is the living encounter with the Lord who transforms life." The *Directory* makes clear that the redeeming love of Christ, saving us from the misery of sin and death, is the heart of all that the Church wants to announce and explain in her catechesis. Everything she teaches is connected to *him* and to his love. Everything in our lives is to flow from our participation in his life, from our being his disciples. All teaching, all witness, all formation and education in the faith, has as its goal assisting others so that they can enter more and more deeply into the life of Christ.

As we step into the *Directory*, then, the Preface and Introduction introduce us to many terms associated with the work of catechesis – *kerygma*, evangelisation, witness, mystagogy, accompaniment – and we will find that their precise meaning and interrelationship is vital to understand if the craft of catechesis we practise is to be successful; but the *Directory* wants us to know at the outset that all of these interlocking terms point to elements in the transmission of the faith that serve a single overarching goal: to deepen and mature our understanding of "the unsearchable riches of Christ", of the "eternal purpose" of God which has been realised in Christ the Lord and to which we now have access through the Holy Spirit who has been given to us.[8] In its conclusion, then, the *Directory* will offer a stirring affirmation of the faith:

> Jesus Christ, Alpha and Omega, is the key of all history. He accompanies every person in order to reveal the love of God. The Crucified and Risen One stands in the middle of the stream of time in order to redeem all of creation and humanity within it. From the pierced side of Jesus crucified, the Holy Spirit is poured out upon the world and the Church is born.[9]

Other phrases that are used in the *Directory* to speak of this goal are "intimate communion with Christ"[10] and "living encounter"[11] with him. Both "communion" and "encounter" speak strongly to the personal nature of the Christian faith, that it is more than a body of truths which is involved. Intellectual grasp of the truth is important, but Christianity offers more – "an ultimate and definitive answer to the question of meaning". It offers an answer to the longing of the heart as well as to the searching of the mind.

John Paul wrote about this unforgettably:

> men and women are on a journey of discovery which is humanly unstoppable – a search for the truth and a search for a person to whom they might entrust themselves. Christian faith comes to meet them, offering the concrete possibility of reaching the goal which they seek.[12]

In Christ, the ultimate truth meets us as a Person; the quest for truth and the quest for a person to whom we might entrust ourselves come together. In his first encyclical, on the love of God, Pope Benedict took up this theme of Christianity offering more than a set of values or ideas:

---

[8] Cf. *Ephesians* 3:8-12.
[9] *Directory for Catechesis* (hereafter *DC*) 427 (references to the *Directory* are given here, as in the case with all Church documents, according to their paragraph number rather than page number).
[10] *DC* 3. This phrase echoes the famous statement of the goal of catechesis given in St John Paul II's *Catechesi Tradendae* (*CT*) 5: "the definitive aim of catechesis is to put people not only in touch but in communion, in intimacy, with Jesus Christ: only he can lead us to the love of the Father in the Spirit and make us share in the life of the Holy Trinity."
[11] *DC* 4.
[12] St John Paul II, *Fides et Ratio* (1998): 33.

Being Christian is not the result of an ethical choice or a lofty idea, but the encounter with an event, a person, which gives life a new horizon and a decisive direction.[13]

The term "encounter" here means more than just "experience". It means that the reality of Christ engages us in and through *the whole of our humanity* – calling for a response from us that involves our mind, senses, imagination and affections; indeed, the whole of our lives. And neither is encounter to be thought of as a single or intermittent matter; the Christian life is a matter of participating in a "culture of encounter"[14] – of Christ enabling us to share more and more deeply in the whole of his life, as members of his Body. The *Directory* is not pointing us, then, to look for isolated "encounter moments", but rather for something much richer and fuller – a way of living in which we come to recognise that Christ has united himself with us "on the Way",[15] sharing in our lives so that we in turn might share in his.[16]

## THE WHOLE CHRIST, HEAD AND MEMBERS

The Person of Christ, then, is the centre of this *Directory*. Inseparably from this, the Preface and Introduction both emphasise *God's faithfulness to his Church*, upholding her so that she can carry the message of life to all the nations. The Introduction reminds us of God's faithfulness across the ages – that this *Directory* is composed in continuity with the explicit command of the risen Christ given just before his ascension, to "proclaim always and everywhere his Gospel".[17] That mission is echoed in the title of the Letter, *Ubicumque et Semper,* by which Benedict XVI established the Pontifical Council for the Promotion of the New Evangelisation, the Council responsible for the new *Directory*.[18] And so we can trace a direct line between the Lord's initial command and this new *Directory*. Christ reminds his apostles straight away after giving his command that

---

[13] Benedict XVI, *Deus Caritas Est* (2005): 1.

[14] *DC* 6.

[15] A classic example of this from the Gospel of St Luke is, of course, Christ's encounter with the disciples on the road to the village of Emmaus. The two disciples, when they realise who Christ is, exclaim, "Did not our hearts burn within us while he talked to us on the road" (24:32). "The road", in the Greek of the New Testament is the same phrase as "the Way", one of the first names given to the group of Christian believers, "followers of the Way" (cf. *Acts* 9:2, 19:9, and so on). Luke the Evangelist is writing about how the risen Christ now meets us on "the Way", in the Christian life.

[16] To emphasise the lifelong nature of this encounter and communion the *Directory* uses the term "accompaniment" (*DC* 3). Jesus "accompanies" us because he is not only the goal we seek but the Way to the goal also.

[17] *DC* 1, referencing *Matthew* 28:19.

[18] Significantly, this Apostolic Letter by Benedict XVI was given on 21st September 2010, the Feast of St Matthew, apostle and evangelist.

their preaching and teaching will be possible because he will be with them: "Lo, I am with you always, to the close of the age."[19]

This promise is more than a vague form of comfort and assurance. God's faithfulness consists in the fact, first of all, that he himself is the Teacher and Saviour of his people. "You call me Teacher and Lord", said Jesus, "and you are right, for so I am."[20] The *Directory* wants us to remember that in catechesis it is above all *God the Blessed Trinity* who teaches, who brings us to the obedience of faith and who leads us more and more deeply into his life. The centrepiece of this *Directory* is a chapter concerned with the Divine "pedagogy" – that is, with God's work of education and redemption.[21] This chapter begins:

> Revelation is the great educational work of God... From the very beginning of salvation history, the Revelation of God manifests itself as an initiative of love, shown in countless moments of careful instruction.[22]

God's faithfulness is shown, then, by his coming among us as Teacher and Saviour. It is also shown in his associating the Church with this work of education, calling her to participate in the healing and salvation of the nations which he has made available.

---

[19] *Matthew* 28:20.
[20] *John* 13:13. Cf. *DC* 161; cf. also *CT* 9.
[21] This is the subject of chapter five of the *Directory*, "The Pedagogy of the Faith".
[22] *DC* 157.

To make this participation in his mission possible the Father gives the Holy Spirit to the Church to enable her to remain rooted in his truth and to communicate unerringly his love to the world. The first apostles, we remember, were instructed to "stay in the city, until you are clothed with power from on high."[23] This clothing with power was realised in the descent of the Holy Spirit, the "the promise of [the] Father" whom Christ would send. And so it is because of God's faithfulness in sending the Spirit that this work of announcing and explaining divine truth continues from generation to generation.

The *Directory*, then, is a sign of God's continuing faithfulness. This is not the first time that the universal Church has issued a *Directory for Catechesis*. Two directories have preceded it: in 1971 (the *General Catechetical Directory*, GCD) and 1997 (the *General Directory for Catechesis*, GDC). The Preface to the new *Directory* notes that this present *Directory* is "situated in dynamic continuity" with the previous directories for catechesis. It is an important point to bear in mind when reading this new *Directory*: this work, as with all Church documents, presumes what has gone before and builds upon the documentary tradition. Some documents of the Magisterium – the teaching office of the Church – reflect this character in the titles they are given: for example, a number of the magisterial documents in the area of the social teaching of the Church are titled simply according to their publication date, reflecting the number of years that have passed since the key founding document of that particular sequence. Thus, Pius XI wrote *Quadragesimo Anno* in 1931, forty years after Leo XIII promulgated *Rerum Novarum* in 1891. St John Paul II wrote an encyclical on Catholic social teaching in 1991 and titled it simply *Centisimus Annus*.

Church documents, then, always *stand in a tradition*, referring back to what was published before, taking and employing key principles from those earlier documents, and consciously referencing and honouring them, seeking to apply their insights to the contemporary situation. We are authentically interpreting any document of the universal Magisterium, such as this work, only when we read it in relation to this living tradition. This asks of us that we attend carefully to the language and terminology of a document, reading it in continuity with how the terms have been employed previously.

On 22nd December 2005, Pope Benedict addressed the Roman Curia on this general point of continuity when he spoke of the importance of an interpreting principle he called "...the 'hermeneutic of reform', of renewal in the continuity of the one subject-Church which the Lord has given to us."[24] He went on to explain how this principle is closely related to the nature of the Church herself: "She is a subject which increases in time and develops, yet always remaining the same, the one subject of the journeying People of God."

---

[23] *Luke* 24:49.

[24] Benedict XVI, *Address to the Roman Curia offering them his Christmas greetings* (22nd December 2005).

When he wrote this, Pope Benedict was addressing the point specifically to the question of how to interpret the place of the Second Vatican Council in relation to the whole of the Church's tradition. Some saw the Council – for good or ill – as a rupture with the past, a new beginning, a starting over and a rejection of tradition. Pope Benedict reminded his audience of this organic image of a *person*: the "one subject-Church...is a subject which increases in time and develops, yet always remaining the same". I am the same subject-Person as I was when I was in the womb and when I was ten years old. I develop, yet always remain the same person. The Church can never embrace a view that involves a break with her past, a denial of Tradition. The Second Vatican Council itself, in its document on the Word of God, writes both of the "Sacred Tradition" and the "living Tradition" of the Church – the one subject-Church is living and her Tradition is holy.[25]

Ensuring that the great ecumenical Councils of the Church,[26] such as the Second Vatican Council, are read and interpreted in continuity with what has gone before is, of course, crucial for the integrity of the Church, and as a witness to God's guarantee of his faithfulness to his Bride, that he will hold her secure in the truth. The hermeneutic of continuity is a vital principle for the catechist to embrace, both in relation to how we understand the Second Vatican Council,[27] and more broadly how we understand the nature of catechesis as a whole. For in fact the work of catechesis can be seen as a supreme example of this principle since it is essentially concerned with the *faithful handing on of all that has been received*. Thus, in the New Testament we see St Paul making this point when he writes, "For I delivered to you as of first importance what I also received..."[28] Paul has received the Gospel from others and he is now handing on that same Gospel. He reminds the Corinthians, to whom he is writing, of "the gospel, which you received, in which you stand, by which you are saved, if you hold it fast..."[29] All of those involved in catechesis participate in the work of the one subject-Church, faithfully handing on to others the fullness of the faith which they themselves have received. The word "catechesis" reminds us of this since it is a word that literally means "echo down", indicating this dynamic of receiving and passing on. The Preface therefore reminds us that "catechesis remains rooted in the solid tradition that has characterised the history of Christianity since its origins."

---

[25] Second Vatican Council, *Dei Verbum* (1965): 9, 12.

[26] "Ecumenical" literally means "universal", from the Greek *oikoumenē*, meaning the world as a single habitation. When used of Church Councils it means that they are universal, that they draw together bishops from across the world.

[27] The Preface reminds us that St Paul VI described the teaching of the Council as the "great Catechism of modern times".

[28] *1 Corinthians* 15:3.

[29] *1 Corinthians* 15:1-2.

## MEETING CHALLENGES WITH FAITH AND INTEGRITY

Reading this *Directory* in continuity with what has preceded it also makes it possible to identify more easily *elements of new emphasis*, of renewed interest. We can ask ourselves: how similar are the three directories on catechesis? In what ways are they different? We know that the three directories for catechesis communicate the same Christian message. At the same time, each has different emphases about *how* to do so, and these emphases reflect the Church's understanding of the "challenges that new times pose for the Church".[30] The *Directory* understands that "Our times are complex, pervaded by profound changes".[31] The challenges are identified as two in particular: "digital culture" and "the globalisation of culture". These two, it says, are profoundly interconnected. The *Directory* will be concerned to explore these two in some depth and to offer ways of catechising in the light of them.

The challenges raised by digital and global culture are summarised here in the Preface: the digital culture, while making information and people more accessible, at the same time takes us away from *reality* into the "virtual", while a global culture which enables us to connect and develop in a more universal fashion, takes us away from the *local* world, the real world in which we live, here and now, as flesh and blood persons. Benefits appear to be conferred. Yet we are at risk of losing real relationships and real connections with people and our environment. And this is a genuine danger for the work of evangelisation and catechesis because "faith, in fact, is transmitted through interpersonal connection and is nourished within the circle of the community." Faith is handed on from *person to person*, in the family, in friendships, in the parish, in the groups and associations to which we belong.

The Church knows, of course, that the Gospel of Christ, since it speaks to the truth of who we are as human beings, can penetrate *every* culture and transform *every* person's life. It is precisely because of this knowledge that the Church knows she must engage with every challenge that people face. The Preface therefore includes a long quotation from the Second Vatican Council's document on bishops on this point, *Christus Dominus*, highlighting the importance of presenting "Christian doctrine in a manner adapted to the needs of the times, that is to say, in a manner that will respond to the difficulties and questions by which people are especially burdened and troubled."[32] Because there is no trouble that falls outside of the concern of Christ and no burden that he is unable to carry, the *Directory* wants to affirm the confidence with which catechists can approach every situation and challenge, ensuring that teaching is clearly addressing the needs and concerns people are expressing so as to "make the faith, as illumined by teaching, a vital, explicit and effective force" in their lives.

---

[30] *DC* 39.
[31] *DC* 38.
[32] Second Vatican Council, *Christus Dominus* (1965): 13.

As well as addressing these challenges of our time, the *Directory* is drawing upon the dynamism of new work in the Church in this area of catechesis. As we noted earlier, this is always undertaken in continuity with what has gone before, as a further development of it, and the Preface reminds us of the key markers that have been laid down since the Second Vatican Council and are sources of potent renewal and ongoing reflection. Especially important are St Paul VI's *Evangelii Nuntiandi* (Evangelisation in the Modern World, 1975) and St John Paul II's *Catechesi Tradendae* (Catechesis in our Time, 1979). More recently we have Pope Francis's *Evangelii Gaudium* (The Gospel of Joy, 2013). These works are powerful documents that continue to shape the Church's thinking. The Preface also reminds us of the *Catechism of the Catholic Church*.[33] It is the ongoing reflection that the Church has been undertaking with regard to her own understanding of catechesis that is ultimately the main driver of this *Directory* and which has occasioned its release. These works, together with much thinking in the Church that has been taking place about catechetics, "have led to achievements that are highly significant for the life of the Church and the maturing of believers, and require a new systematic presentation."

---

[33] A whole chapter, chapter six, will be dedicated to that work of the universal Church. For now, it is enough to say that directories of catechesis differ from the *Catechism* in a vital respect: the former are less concerned with questions of the content of the faith, and more with *principles of transmission*, with how the faith is handed on and received. In relation to this present *Directory*, therefore, the *Catechism* remains the stable reference point with regard to the content of the faith, with what the Scriptures call the "deposit of faith" (cf. *1 Timothy* 6:20).

We will be analysing this thinking as it is unpacked in the following chapters, but a brief summary can be given here. The key point is the emphasis placed on evangelisation as the context for catechesis.[34] This is certainly not a new point. Nonetheless we can say that there is a strong attempt here to trace the *implications* of this view into the way in which one thinks about all aspects of catechesis and especially perhaps the formation of catechists. One way in which this affects the delivery of the content of the faith is a consistent focus on the importance of what the Church calls the "first announcement", or "first proclamation" (in Greek, *kerygma*). Another way this affects catechesis is in the attention given to the person of the catechist as a living witness to the faith. The unity between faith and life in the catechist is one of the hallmarks of this *Directory*, which does not want to focus just on what catechists *do*, but more especially on who they *are*. Because of this it brings the question of the spirituality of the catechist to the forefront. The Preface concludes in this way:

> Holiness is the crucial word that can be pronounced in presenting a new *Directory for Catechesis*. It is the herald of a way of life that catechists are also called to follow with constancy and fidelity. They are not alone on this demanding journey. The Church, in every part of the world, can present models of catechists who have attained holiness and even martyrdom in living their ministry every day. Their witness is fruitful, and makes it still thinkable in our time that each of us can persevere in this adventure even in the silent, laborious, and sometimes thankless work of *being* a catechist.

## QUESTIONS FOR REFLECTION

1   How convinced am I that my ministry is fruitful only in so far as I am dependent on Christ and on the grace that he provides?

2   How do I express this conviction in the time I give to prayer and to the study of the Scriptures and the teaching of the Church?

---

[34] "The close connection between evangelisation and catechesis therefore becomes the distinctive feature of this *Directory*." (Preface)

## A Prayer for Catechists

GOD OUR FATHER,
You have called us into your service
To help others to know you
and to learn how to receive your infinite love.
Give us the grace to know this love in our own lives
That we may bear witness to you and speak well of you.
We ask this in the name of your only Son,
Our Lord and Saviour, Jesus Christ.
Amen.

# CHAPTER I:

# Revelation and its Transmission

With this chapter of the *Directory* we enter into a discussion of the *universal principles* that guide the Church's work of catechesis today. The *Directory* takes a clear and systematic approach to discussing this: chapter one describes the *content* of catechesis, which is God's revelation of himself, and explains how catechesis finds its fruitful setting within evangelisation. It then moves on in chapter two to study the *nature of catechesis* itself in detail. Then it moves to the question of who the *catechist* is (chapter three) and finally what kind of *formation* is needed to transmit the content (chapter four).

The title of the part, "Catechesis in the Church's mission of evangelisation", provides us with the main theme to be explored: evangelisation as the context for catechesis. As we have already seen, this central theme is not a new one. A close connection between catechesis and evangelisation was already identified in the first General *Directory* in 1971.[35] This connection then played a major part in the content and structure of the 1997 *Directory*; in fact, part one of that 1997 *Directory* has the same title as is found here. When the current *Directory* says that this connection is "the distinctive feature of this *Directory*"[36] we must understand, then, that it is speaking of a further intensification of this trajectory, a point of strong

---

[35] There it states, "In every case, ...one must keep in mind that the element of conversion is always present in the dynamism of faith, and for that reason any form of catechesis must also perform the role of evangelisation." (*GCD* 18)
[36] *DC* Preface.

continuity with what precedes it which is now more systematically consolidated and elaborated.

## THE ULTIMATE FOUNDATION

The *Directory* describes the purpose of this chapter and those of this first part of the *Directory* as providing the "foundations". *Everything* in the rest of the *Directory* will be built on what is presented in this part. The opening paragraph of this chapter expresses the main thought succinctly and powerfully:

> All that the Church is, all that the Church does, finds its ultimate foundation in the fact that God, in his goodness and wisdom, wanted to reveal the mystery of his will by communicating himself to human beings.[37]

Notice the emphatic statement here: "all that the Church *is*", "all that the Church *does*" – everything we need to understand about the *nature* of the Church and everything we need to understand about her *activity*, including the activity of evangelisation and catechesis, is found in one glorious reality: that the good and wise Lord has willed to reveal himself, to communicate himself to us.

It is easy to think of Revelation simply as God choosing to tell us *about* many different things – about the importance of Baptism, about the ordained priesthood, about people and events in the Bible, about how to act to secure justice, and so on. Catechesis is then understood to be concerned with learning these things and handing them on to others to learn. God's Revelation is seen mainly as a rich and varied list of beliefs and guidance for action. Though this is not all that the Church wants to say about Revelation, there is obviously truth in this view, and in no way does the *Directory* desire to play down the importance of learning the truths God has revealed to guide our understanding and our lives.

But if we were to stop there we would be in danger of missing the *point* of it all, the reason *why* God reveals. The Church has always focused us upon the *purpose* of Revelation. The *Directory* follows the *Catechism* here in choosing to provide a quotation from the Second Vatican Council, from the Dogmatic Constitution on Divine Revelation, *Dei Verbum,* to explain this purpose: all that has been revealed is for the sake of giving us "access to the Father" and so that we can "come to share in the divine nature".[38] The point of learning and teaching the truths of Revelation is that they lead us to the One God, Father, Son and Holy Spirit, the God who is the Truth. Just as in our human relationships the point of getting to know many things about a person and learning how to enjoy his company and act well towards him is

---

[37] *DC* 11.

[38] *DC* 12, quoting here from Second Vatican Council's Dogmatic Constitution on Divine Revelation, *Dei Verbum* (1965): 2. The *Catechism* presents the purpose of Revelation using this same passage in *CCC* 51.

for the sake of *a life with that person*, so all of our striving to learn and hand on the truths of the faith is for the sake of helping ourselves and others into the happiness of *being* with God.

There is more to be said about Revelation. It is not only that God has revealed truths about himself which lead us to him. He has not simply communicated messages of truth through an emissary, and given us access to himself in this way. He has not only engraved words of truth on our hearts, or sent ambassadors to announce who he is. Yes, he has done all of those things. But there is something more. The *Directory* here chooses to quote Pope Benedict: "God has shown himself. In person."[39] God has revealed *himself*. The point of it all, the end of our strivings, the life of perfect happiness, the face of love, has not remained at a distance, at the end of a journey to be taken, but has assumed our flesh and taken our nature so that we can know him and hold fast to him. This is the "novelty" of the Christian faith, that Christianity is rooted not in a set of ideas but in a *fact*: God has revealed himself.[40] This opening section of the chapter, then, reminds us of this, providing us with our fundamental orientation, our ultimate foundation.

## THE BATTLE

Everything in the Church is rooted in this theme of God's appearing among us to show himself so that we can live with him forever. The heart of the Christian proclamation is therefore one of great beauty, great attractiveness. The *Directory* quotes from an early Father, aptly named "golden tongue" because of his ability to communicate the beauty of the faith in his speech: "What news is more beautiful than this? God on earth and man in heaven!"[41]

The urgency and grace of this proclamation flows also from something else: the fact that it is announced as a word of victory in a world of bitter hatred and struggle, a word of beauty in the face of the ugliness of sin and anguish of death,[42] and a word of love in a world troubled by mutual accusation and deep self-hatred. The Christian proclamation is that "God is with us to free us from the darkness of sin and death".[43] God reveals himself in order to *liberate* us and save us from evil.[44] And so the *Directory* is marked with a powerful sense of appeal in its pages, calling us urgently to *mission*, to *show mercy* and to do all we can to enter into *dialogue* with others for the sake of this salvation.[45]

---

[39] *DC* 13, quoting from Benedict XVI, *Verbum Domini* (2010): 92.

[40] *DC* 13.

[41] St John Chrysostom (c.347-407), quoted in *DC* 13.

[42] Cf. the powerful paragraph in *DC* 107, for example.

[43] *DC* 12, quoting Second Vatican Council, *Dei Verbum* (1965): 4.

[44] Cf. *DC* 14, 30.

[45] Cf. the final three themes of this chapter: the missionary "going forth" (49-50), the framework of mercy (51-52) and the "laboratory" of dialogue (53-54).

The Gospels present Christ's life as a great battle against evil, as he confronts and is victorious over the devil who has thrown himself across God's plans, seeking to cripple and entangle the human person in a web of deceit and lies.[46] This biblical understanding was summed up in the final document of the Second Vatican Council:

> The whole of man's history has been the story of dour combat with the powers of evil, stretching, so our Lord tells us, from the very dawn of history until the last day. Finding himself in the midst of the battlefield man has to struggle to do what is right, and it is at great cost to himself, and aided by God's grace, that he succeeds in achieving his own inner integrity.[47]

Jesus reminds his disciples that when he speaks his saving word Satan immediately seeks to rob people of this.[48] And yet the power of Christ's word is such that it can be richly fruitful if, by grace, the heart of the recipient is open. The work of evangelisation, then, is the scene of *spiritual battle*[49] which asks of his disciples prayer, fasting, and the witness of a committed and personal love which can touch the heart of the other.[50]

## EVANGELISATION

We can see why the Church's understanding of evangelisation is so much more than a matter of speaking a message. It is indeed proclaiming the word of hope to sustain us in the midst of the battle.[51] But it is more than this. It is *making Christ present*. The *Directory* describes it this way: evangelisation is making the "enduring presence of Christ concrete, in such a way that those who draw near to the Church may encounter in his person the way to 'save their lives' (cf. *Matthew* 16:25) and open themselves to a new horizon".[52] And again, "Evangelising is...concerned with bringing about the presence and proclamation of Jesus Christ".[53] Giving the message is inseparable from giving the Person.

---

[46] Cf. *Matthew* 4:1-11; *John* 8:43-44; *1 John* 5:19; cf. *1 Peter* 5:8.

[47] Second Vatican Council, *Gaudium et Spes* (1965): 37.

[48] *Mark* 4:15.

[49] Cf. *Luke* 10:17-19.

[50] Cf. *DC* 76, and for Jesus's reminder about fasting and prayer, *Mark* 9:29.

[51] Cf. *Isaiah* 50:4: "The Lord God has given me the tongue of those who are taught, that I may know how to sustain with a word him that is weary."

[52] *DC* 29.

[53] *DC* 29. Thus the statement that "evangelising is not, in the first place, the delivery of a doctrine; but rather, making present and announcing Jesus Christ" is not a downplaying of the teaching, the doctrine, of the Church, but rather a call to allow his teaching to *lead one* into his Presence. Cf. also *DC* 18 on the way in which faith is a threefold movement of "believing that", "believing Jesus" and "believing 'in' Jesus".

Let us look at why this must be the case. God's purpose in creating was to make creatures in his image and likeness, able to share in his life. When those creatures wounded and disfigured themselves through a failure to trust, deceived into seeking their growth and safety through isolating themselves from the very Source of their life, God chose to draw near to them in his own Person, reaching out to them to share his mercy and the offer of eternal life. All that he said and did was for the purpose of eliciting *trust* in himself so that his creatures might not fear to put themselves into his hands.[54]

What is at stake in evangelisation, then, is the salvation of the person – that we might become sharers in God's own life and nature. In giving us himself, God also offers us *ourselves*, asking us to receive from him ourselves as new beings, with a new life, a life clothed in his own. The work of evangelisation is to bring others to a place of trust and openness in their lives where they can receive this. And this is a work requiring presence and stability and accompaniment by the Church – key themes in this document – because we have wandered so far from the land of the true likeness to God that our return is felt like a death as well as offering us glimpses of the new life. (The next chapter, on the nature of catechesis, will explain how our proclamation *must*, therefore, centre on the death and resurrection of Christ.)

What is the role of the human evangelist and catechist in this process? The next chapter will begin to unfold the answer to that question. Meanwhile, however, it is right that we ask: how can anyone but God himself give us his life, give us back to ourselves renewed and purified? Surely the God who created us is the only One who can re-create us. This is so, and thus this chapter of the *Directory* underscores that it is the Son and the Spirit, like two "hands" of the Father, who shape and remould us to make us able to bear the weight of God's glory.[55] We can see this truth unfolded for us very clearly in the archetypal moment of evangelisation: the annunciation of God's salvation to the Blessed Virgin.[56] The angel Gabriel appears here as God's messenger, the one "sent from God", the evangeliser (and it is helpful that "angel" is clearly at the heart of the word e*vangel*isation to remind us of this fact). He speaks the promise, proclaims the word of hope: "you will conceive in your womb and bear a son, and you shall call his name Jesus". Evangelisation is both a *message* of hope and also a *gift* to be received, a new life to be received, a life whose name is "God saves". That this life is able to be given and received is made possible only by the overshadowing of the Holy Spirit. Here we see, then, the Trinitarian act of evangelisation, the *making present* of Christ the *Word* in the flesh of the Virgin.[57]

---

[54] Cf. *DC* 4, 18, 39, 172, 179. For Jesus's striking appeal in this regard, cf. *Luke* 12:32.

[55] *DC* 22. Cf. also *CCC* 704, 737.

[56] *Luke* 1:26-38. Cf. *DC* 159.

[57] The primacy of God's work in evangelisation and catechesis is captured in a phrase that the *Directory* will employ a good deal: "the primacy of grace". (*DC* 33)

The gift of the new life of Christ immediately inspires the Blessed Virgin to set out "with haste" to make him present to her cousin Elizabeth, to proclaim God's goodness, and to lovingly accompany her in the final stages of her own pregnancy.[58] We can see from these episodes from Luke's opening chapter how evangelisation is indeed what the *Directory* teaches us: "a reality that is 'rich, complex and dynamic', and in its development incorporates various possibilities: witness and proclamation, word and sacrament, inner change and social transformation."[59]

## THE RESPONSE OF FAITH

The narrative of the annunciation is also helpful to us when reflecting upon the section on the *nature of faith* in this chapter.[60] In addition to works by St Augustine and St Thomas the *Directory* here refers us to St John Paul II's Encyclical Letter on faith and

---

[58] Cf. *Luke* 1:39-56.
[59] *DC* 16, citing St Paul VI, Evangelisation in the Modern World, *Evangelii Nuntiandi* (1975): 17.
[60] *DC* 17-21.

reason, *Fides et Ratio*, and Pope Francis's first encyclical, on the "Light of Faith".[61] It also takes us to the *Catechism*. These magisterial documents share the perspective that Mary perfectly embodies what the Church calls "the obedience of faith" and the current *Directory* will return to this point, with the final paragraph of the whole text reminding us of this:

> Always shining upon the Church's joyful task of evangelisation is Mary, the Mother of the Lord, who in complete docility to the action of the Holy Spirit was able to listen to and welcome into herself the word of God, becoming 'the purest realisation of faith'. (*CCC* 148)[62]

We turn to the Blessed Virgin, then, to understand the act of faith that is sought by all who evangelise and catechise. The phrase "obedience of faith" reminds us that, just as it was in Mary's case, so always faith is inseparable from action: hearing the Word leads to doing. In speaking his word God calls forth from us not only an assent to what he reveals and a close adherence to him but also a "following in his footsteps along the way". "It is an adherence of the heart, of the mind, and of action".[63]

We said earlier that only God can give us his life. That is his work. The response of faith is also the work of God. A recurring attentiveness in the *Directory* is to the action of the Holy Spirit. Paragraph 23 puts it this way:

> The Holy Spirit, true protagonist of the whole ecclesial mission, acts both in the Church and in those whom she must reach and by whom, in a certain way, she must also be reached, since God works in the heart of everyone. The Holy Spirit continues to enliven the Church, which lives by the word of God, and makes her grow always in the understanding of the Gospel, sending her and supporting her in the work of evangelising the world. The Spirit himself, from within humanity, sows the seed of the Word; supports good desires and works; prepares the reception of the Gospel and grants faith, so that, through the Church's witness, human beings may recognise the loving presence and communication of God.

The Holy Spirit acts in the Church's mission both in those who transmit the faith and in those who receive it. If we look at the Scriptures we will see in fact that it is the Holy Spirit's work in the one *receiving* the Word that is the focus. Thus, for example, when St Paul is writing to the Corinthian church he says, "I planted, Apollos watered,

---

[61] The encyclical of Francis is also the final encyclical of Benedict XVI, in his trio on the theological virtues of love, hope and faith. Thus in this section of the *Directory* we see a happy uniting of three recent pontificates.

[62] *DC* 428. In *Lumen Fidei* we find, "In the fullness of time, God's word was spoken to Mary and she received that word into her heart, her entire being, so that in her womb it could take flesh and be born as light for humanity" (58) while in *Fides et Ratio* we find the emphasis placed on the freedom of that perfect assent (108).

[63] *DC* 18.

but God gave the growth. So neither he who plants nor he who waters is anything, but only God who gives the growth."[64] The work of the Holy Spirit is above all that of *preparing* the one who is to receive the word of life, for if there was no *capacity* to receive the divine Word the mission of teaching and of bringing Christ to the nations would make no sense.[65]

The work of evangelisation – its transmission and its reception, belongs to God. Only God gives the growth. Only under the power of the Holy Spirit does faith take shape in a person's life. In almost every paragraph of this section this essential truth is affirmed. But this does not mean that God acts alone or independently of his creatures. In fact, the opposite is the case. God's taking flesh to live with us was precisely for the sake of giving us the ability to share in his divine life. We are to be brought into union with him. We are given the privilege of being true actors in the divine play.

This unity of God and the human person in making a response of faith is emphasised in another paragraph in this section on faith where the vital place of both faith *and* reason is stressed.[66] Faith does not bypass or denigrate our reason. The Christian faith in God in fact underpins our confidence that our reason is trustworthy and that the universe is an ordered whole that can be explored by the mind and uncovered through scientific investigation. And so the *Directory* will go on to affirm the value of rational discovery and scientific work.[67] It is an important point for the *Directory* to make early on since so many whom the Church seeks to evangelise are tempted into a belief that religion and rationality, faith and science must be at odds.[68]

Importantly, the *Directory* also speaks of faith being born "from the maternal womb",[69] a beautifully Marian image that here refers to the Church our mother. The *Directory* having emphasised, then, the divine activity in the transmission of the faith it is now reminding us that God always associates his Bride the Church with this action. Faith is transmitted and sustained by God *and* his Church. The response of faith is never a solitary act (though it is a deeply *personal* one). Every act of faith is a participation in "the ecclesial faith that always comes before [us]." The *Directory* could not be more emphatic on this point: "The faith of the disciple of Christ is therefore kindled, sustained, and transmitted only in the communion of ecclesial faith".[70]

---

[64] *1 Corinthians* 3:6-7.

[65] For this point about the Holy Spirit's work of preparation of people to receive the Word cf. *CCC* 722 and 1093-1098.

[66] *DC* 19.

[67] Cf. *DC* 354-358.

[68] *DC* 355.

[69] *DC* 21. The image is used repeatedly in the *Directory* to remind us of our always being held and nurtured in our faith by the Church: 64d, 110, 131, 133, 262a.

[70] *DC* 21.

## THE PROCESS OF EVANGELISATION

The *Directory* next proceeds to make clearer what it means by saying that evangelisation is concerned with bringing about the proclamation and the person of Jesus Christ. This takes place not as a once-for-all event. Receiving Christ and his message happens over time. The *Directory*, as we have seen, uses the image of "seeds of the Word"[71] and this may remind us of the famous parable of Christ of the sower scattering the seeds.[72] If we think of the soils into which the seed fell as a progressive series – moving from the hard earth, to a shallow, rocky soil and then to a more receptive depth but where the good growth of the seed is threatened by competing weeds, and finally to the rich, fertile soil – then we will have a sense of what the *Directory* wants to communicate here by the notion of evangelisation as a *process*. The seed that is sown gradually takes root and becomes established until it is at last able to yield its harvest. That takes time, and there are threats accompanying its growth – the birds of the air, the burning sun, the strangling weeds. The soil needs preparation and nutrition so that the seed can develop. The process of evangelisation presented here describes how the Church sustains, protects and nurtures the growth of faith, providing "nourishment for the spiritual growth of each person or community".[73]

Just as Jesus's parable has the seed passing through different stages, so the process of evangelisation here is described as made up of "various stages and moments" and the *Directory* says that we can think of these stages as sequential and also as "aspects of the process".[74] That sounds a little obscure but in fact it simply reflects the complexity of who we are. If we think about the process of learning, we would probably say that we learn best when things are presented in a certain order, with points building on one another. But we might also agree that we often need to go back to remind ourselves of earlier points and principles. It is not simply a linear process. Even more is this the case in the process of learning to love another person: here there is also a certain order we could in principle set out – of acquaintance and growing knowledge, friendship, courtship, marriage, and finally growing old together. But how complex that path can be, with the elements of friendship needing maturing, with knowledge of oneself and the other person often taking place largely *after* marriage, with the loss and recovery of that "first love",[75] and so on. There are stages, but the process is not simply a matter of leaving behind earlier points.

The process is described as having three broad phases, described as "missionary action", "catechetical-initiatory" action and "pastoral action".[76] You will notice the

---

[71] Cf. *DC* 23, 332, 333, 350.

[72] *Mark* 4:1-9.

[73] *DC* 32.

[74] *DC* 32.

[75] Cf. *Revelation* 2:4.

[76] *DC* 33-35.

many footnotes in this section that refer us to the Church's *Rite of Christian Initiation of Adults* (RCIA). This process of evangelisation, in other words, is not merely a theoretical presentation: it is the process followed when the Church brings new converts into full communion with her life. The *Directory* provides us with the terms for these stages that are used in the RCIA: "pre-catechumenate", "catechumenate" (together with "purification and enlightenment") and "mystagogy".

One other feature that it is important to note about this process of evangelisation is that we can identify three strands running through each of the phases, strands that we can broadly describe as catechetical, liturgical and pastoral. These are woven together to provide an integrated and unified experience of the faith for the one being evangelised. So, for example, in the description of the second phase the *Directory* writes of "catechesis, together with [the] liturgical ceremonies, works of charity, and experience of fraternity"[77] being bound together in the spiritual journey of the catechumen. Overall, this unity of those dimensions or strands, set out in phases, is what the *Directory* calls the "catechumenal model", which it says is urgently needed as a source of inspiration for all catechesis. In the next chapter, we will see how the *Directory* unpacks this point, asking not for a slavish imitation of it so much as "taking on its style and its formative dynamism".[78]

---

[77] *DC* 34.
[78] *DC* 64.

## A NEW EVANGELISATION

The final section of this chapter focuses on what the Church means by the "new evangelisation". This is, of course, particularly pertinent since the whole of the work of catechesis was placed by Pope Benedict under the Pontifical Council for the Promotion of the New Evangelisation. In what does this "newness" consist? It is tempting to think of it solely in relation to the situation in which the Church finds herself culturally, especially in the European and American continents, the situation of widespread cultural apostasy, of the rejection of the faith among sectors of the populations of formerly strong Christian countries. Secularism, communism, atheism and religious indifference have each made significant inroads into areas where there are rich Christian traditions and have brought alien perspectives that have deeply damaged Christian formation in these cultures. The *Directory* references[79] the urgent call of St Paul VI and St John Paul II for a response to this situation. St John Paul went so far as to say that "the moment has come to commit all of the Church's energies to a new evangelisation and to the mission *ad gentes*."[80] And he added, "No believer in Christ, no institution of the Church can avoid this supreme duty: to proclaim Christ to all peoples." A clarion call went out for the Church to commit herself wholly to mission in the light of this situation.

The *Directory* helps us into a fuller perspective at this point, to understand better what the popes were asking for. The call to a new evangelisation needs to be placed in the context of the Second Vatican Council, the first Church Council to be dedicated wholly to the theme of pastoral and catechetical mission. Calling for a universal Council dedicated to this, St John XXIII associated the Council with the theme of Pentecost,[81] the great feast of the Holy Spirit's outpouring upon the Church and her move to universal mission. Thus the new evangelisation is especially concerned with the work of the Holy Spirit:

> The Holy Spirit is the soul of the evangelising Church. For this reason the call for a new evangelisation has less to do with the dimension of time as with making all moments of the process of evangelisation ever more open to the renewing action of the Spirit of the Risen One.[82]

More important than a focus on the time we live in is the focus on the activity of the Holy Spirit. There are certainly new times and new challenges, but this calls the Church primarily to the necessity to *trust* and to foster *a spirituality of self-gift* for the sake of bringing Christ's saving work to the world.[83]

---

79 *DC* 39, note 33.
80 *RM* 3.
81 This link was made in his announcement of the Council on 25th January 1959, and the theme was taken up in many subsequent addresses.
82 *DC* 39.
83 Cf. *DC* 39-40.

The phrase used in the *Directory* to describe the stance called for, for "every one of the baptised" is that of being a "missionary disciple".[84] It is an interesting phrase for the accent is on the noun "disciple" which is modified by the adjective "missionary". The fundamental call to the baptised in the new evangelisation, in other words, is to *discipleship*, to staying close to Christ the Source of our lives. It is to dwell as branches in Christ the Vine, without whom we can do nothing.[85] Writing of the Church, the *Directory* puts it this way:

> ...in this mission of hers "she begins by being evangelised herself. She is the community of believers, the community of hope lived and communicated, the community of brotherly love, and she needs to listen unceasingly to what she must believe, to her reasons for hope, to the new commandment of love...she has a constant need of being evangelised, if she wishes to retain her freshness, vigour and strength in order to proclaim the Gospel."[86]

The call is to remain in the Vine, staying rooted there, because there we discover the infinite love of Christ who is the One who was "sent" from the Father for the salvation of the world.[87] It is from him that we receive our mission. This is why catechesis is "at the service of the new evangelisation"[88] since catechesis forms the baptised for that intimacy with Christ which allows them to know his heart and thus participate in the Church in her "sending" of them to others who have not yet met and come to know him. The Church knows that without this *drawing in* to Christ, mission would be an empty gesture. Without the personal knowledge of the love of Christ for oneself and without the conviction that he really *is* the truth that others need, "mission" is reduced to a human activity bereft of the power of the Holy Spirit. But when there is this confident *rootedness* in Christ, mission can occur. The true Centre of our lives, Christ himself, holds us in our mission.

Catechesis, then, has a key role to play in the formation of disciples for mission, forming disciples who are to "participate actively in the proclamation of the Gospel and to make the kingdom of God present in the world".[89] They can be formed as people of mercy and dialogue, learning how to undertake "a pastoral dialogue without

---

[84] *DC* 40. This phrase, explored by Benedict XVI, is also a strong feature in Francis's Apostolic Exhortation, *Evangelii Gaudium*. For Benedict XVI on this cf. Brad Bursa, "'Being With' vs. 'Being Sent': Missionary Discipleship in the Writing of Pope Benedict XVI", *The Catechetical Review*, Vol.3.2, 5-7.

[85] *John* 15:5. The word "remain" is used by Jesus ten times in this short passage on the disciples as branches in the vine.

[86] *DC* 28, citing *EN* 15.

[87] For example, cf. *John* 3:17, 4:34, 5:36-37, and so on. Jesus is the One who is sent by the Father.

[88] *DC* 48.

[89] *DC* 50.

relativism, which does not negotiate one's Christian identity, but which seeks to reach the heart of the other".[90] Centred on Christ, and well-formed catechetically, the Christian in mission can learn the difficult art which the *Directory* wants of them, to know how to distinguish *truth* from custom and focus upon Christ's kingdom which transcends every earthly gain.[91] Then the "sure and immutable" doctrine of the faith can reinvigorate every culture.[92]

The absolutely crucial heart and centre of the new evangelisation, then, is that of enabling every person to have "personal access to the encounter with Christ".[93] The *Directory* urges us to realise the importance of this priority since, reading the "signs of the times", it notes that we face a world in which the phenomenon of globalisation, together with mass media and the central role being given to science and technology is associated with priority being given to "the outward, the immediate, the visible, the quick, the superficial and the provisional".[94] Personal identity and freedom are threatened by this "vast cultural transformation".[95] The crisis is, above all, in one's self-understanding, and only the encounter with Christ can restore a person to themselves. Catechesis and evangelisation is therefore a profound form of mercy: "Catechetical action, in fact, consists in offering the possibility of escaping the greatest form of ignorance, which prevents people from knowing their own identity and vocation."[96]

## QUESTIONS FOR REFLECTION

1 How is Jesus asking me for an act of faith today, at this *moment*?

2 In what areas am I holding back from an assent of faith?

3 What areas of my *life* and my *ministry* do I need to trustingly hand over to him?

---

[90] *DC* 54, quoting from Francis.

[91] On this, cf. the Preface where St Turibius of Mogrovejo's saying, "Christ is truth, not custom" is used to explain how Christianity can penetrate any culture in a way that avoids all relativism. Cf. also *DC* 43 on how evangelisation must avoid thinking in terms of "territory".

[92] *DC* 44.

[93] *DC* 48.

[94] *DC* 46, quoting *EG* 62. And for this analysis cf. *DC* 42-47.

[95] *DC* 47.

[96] *DC* 52.

# A Prayer for Catechists

LORD JESUS CHRIST,
You are the fullness of the revelation of the Father
    and of his love.
You are the Way in which we walk, day by day,
The Truth that gives us stability,
And the Life that provides the happiness we seek.
Help us to receive you in our lives
As the Saviour we need in every situation,
And witness faithfully to you in our words and actions.
We ask this in your precious name.
Amen.

# CHAPTER II:

# The Identity of Catechesis

The second chapter of the *Directory* is set out in five sections:

- The nature of catechesis
- Catechesis in the process of evangelisation
- The goals of catechesis
- The tasks of catechesis
- Sources of catechesis

One can see a sensible progression in the chapter. It begins by asking what something *is*, for when one knows its nature then other questions about it can be asked, such as "where does something with this nature fit into the wider picture?" The relationship of goals to tasks is that of ends and means to that end so again it makes sense to treat those sections in that order. Finally, there is a lengthy section on the sources of catechesis: from where does catechesis draw its *life*?

## THE NATURE OF CATECHESIS AND ITS PLACE WITHIN EVANGELISATION

Two paragraphs introduce this question of the nature of catechesis, nos. 55-56. Paragraph 55 begins by drawing our attention to the etymology of the word: catechesis comes from the Greek *katechein* which means "resound". The first, and most important, thing to know about catechesis is what is contained in the word itself – that it is an *echo*. If catechesis is an echo then it is natural to ask: an echo of *what*? Or, an echo of *who*? The opening sentence gives us the answer to those two questions:

> Catechesis is an ecclesial act, arising from the missionary mandate of the Lord (cf. *Matthew* 28:19-20) and aimed, as its very name indicates, at making the proclamation of his passion, death and resurrection continually resound in the heart of every person, so that his life may be transformed.

The "who" is the Lord himself and the "what" is his passion, death and resurrection.

The answers to these questions, then, are stunning, and it is easy to realise why the work of catechesis is held in such awe in the Church. The echo is of the *God-Man himself* and of *his dying and rising*. That is, in sum, the nature of catechesis, to provide a faithful echo of this.

This understanding will affect, clearly, everything about the goals, tasks and sources of catechesis, and it will also affect how we are to think of ourselves as catechists (chapter three) and how catechists are formed (chapter four). What is it to *be* an echo of Christ and the mystery of his passion, death and resurrection? How can I be *formed* to be this?

We should not run quickly over the opening phrase of this sentence either: "Catechesis is an *ecclesial* act". As a catechist I am formed to be an echo within the heart of the Church which has received this command from the Lord. I receive my mandate from the Church which has echoed it down to me, which has faithfully handed on to me what I have received. I catechise within the "echo" of the Church. At this point we can remind ourselves of everything that the Preface and Introduction to the *Directory* have communicated to us in this respect.

The next part of this opening paragraph tries to capture something of the "richness" of the essence of catechesis, of what it means to echo Christ in his paschal mystery. It entails the "harmonious integration" of a number of elements: "accompaniment, education, and formation in the faith and for the faith, an introduction to the celebration of the Mystery, illumination and interpretation of human life and history." What do we learn from this?

- It is *personal* and *extended over time* (accompaniment), an echo that continually resounds in the lives of others and not a once-and-for-all event
- It provides others with an *understanding* of Christ and his saving work for us (education)
- It offers *both a cognitive and a broader shaping of the person* to build the person up in faith (formation in the faith and for the faith), providing a way of understanding themselves and the whole of human history (illumination and interpretation of human life and history)
- It *points to where Christ in his fullness is to be found*, in the sacraments, and especially the Mass (an introduction to the celebration of the Mystery).

Paragraph 56 is a very interesting one. It pins down the nature of catechesis more precisely by relating it to the first proclamation on the one hand and to ongoing formation on the other. Here it is already anticipating the discussion in section 2 of the chapter, on the place of catechesis within the mission of evangelisation, for evangelisation is made up of a series of "phases" or "moments" – pre-evangelisation, first proclamation, catechesis and ongoing formation as the most important. Catechesis has its own place *within this overall mission*. It "promotes the processes of initiation, growth, and maturation of the faith". Catechesis is concerned with helping one who has faith into its maturing. Paragraphs 69-72 walk us through the characteristics of catechesis, helping us to distinguish this moment from those which surround it.

In the first place, catechesis is particularly *closely united to the sacraments of initiation* – Baptism, Confirmation and the Eucharist. These sacraments "establish the foundations of Christian life" and make up a single unity, with the Eucharist as the centre and goal.[97] It is entirely appropriate that catechists should concern themselves with preparing candidates for these sacraments as a central part of their work, whether for adults or for children. Catechesis aims at ensuring that these foundations for the Christian life are in place. Moreover, it is not only preparation for the reception of the sacraments with which catechesis is concerned, but helping candidates to understand how the sacraments are themselves the preparation needed for the Christian life itself, launching them into "sacramental mission".[98]

---

[97] *DC 70.*
[98] *DC 69.*

In the second place, *the whole character of "harmonious integration" is spelled out*: catechesis focuses on being "basic, essential, organic, systematic and integral formation".[99] These epithets signal the way in which catechesis is a loving service to the learner – it provides what is basic and essential, the foundations of the faith; it builds on those foundations securely and systematically, providing an ordered account of the learning to be acquired, not being haphazard or tangential; and it is organic, uniting the elements of learning into a satisfying whole, overcoming fragmentation. All of these elements together ensure an integral formation – a unified formation that has wholeness and completeness.

Thirdly, *summaries of the faith* are mentioned and the notion of "harmonious understanding" is repeated again. Summaries draw together elements into a unified whole, identifying the essential points. In the catechetical process the *Our Father* as a summary of prayer, the creeds as summaries of faith and the Commandments as a summary of Christian living are core components of what is delivered in catechesis.[100]

These points are drawn together in a concise way in the *Directory* which sums up the particular contribution of catechesis in the work of evangelisation:

> Catechesis is placed at the service of the believer's response of faith, enabling him to live the Christian life in a state of conversion. This is in essence a matter of fostering the internalisation of the Christian message.[101]

Catechesis enters the process of evangelisation to serve and deepen the state of conversion to Christ by enabling an "internalisation" of the faith – by enabling it to take secure root in life so that it is well integrated into the whole of one's life.

Now that we have identified more closely the unique nature of catechesis, we can return to paragraph 56. The interesting point is that, while acknowledging the specific character of catechesis the emphasis is definitely on ensuring that catechists do not think of their work in a watertight compartment. When we consider the catechesis is a moment in a process of evangelisation – prefaced by pre-evangelisation and first proclamation and completed in ongoing formation – we should recognise that "it is no longer possible to stress such differences". Catechesis is the *centre* of evangelisation, the great work of providing the foundation blocks for the Christian life, providing for an internalisation of the faith and an integration of the faith in to life. But the boundary points with what goes before and after are porous. Catechesis must *hold the centre* and be *closely united* to both and constantly *bear both in mind*. The *Directory* explains what happens if catechists neglect to do this: on the one hand, the first proclamation has no effective follow up to deepen and mature faith, and when this happens the person

---

[99] *DC* 71.
[100] This is why, together with the sacraments, these constitute the heart of the *Catechism of the Catholic Church*, as the substance of what is to be handed on in catechesis.
[101] *DC* 73.

is robbed of an understanding of the faith, that "new horizon of life that is opened wide". And on the other hand, people who come asking for an ongoing formation have often not yet received an "explicit experience of faith" or "know its power and warmth". Standing at the centre point, catechists need to deliver their catechesis in such a way as to encourage the full process of evangelisation to be received by those who approach.

## THE *KERYGMA* AND CATECHESIS

The *Directory* now offers a lengthy focus on the *keryyrna*.[102] The word is taken from the Greek and means a public proclamation or announcement,[103] while the one who gives this is the *keryx*, the herald. The *kerygma* can be distinguished from the "rich essence" of catechesis by virtue of its concentration on the most essential heart of the faith and the intention of proclaiming this so as to elicit an initial response of faith in the hearer.

What does the *Directory* see as the content of the proclamation, the *kerygma*? It begins by quoting from Pope Francis's *Evangelii Gaudium*:

> The *kerygma* is trinitarian. The fire of the Spirit is given in the form of tongues and leads us to believe in Jesus Christ who, by his death and resurrection, reveals and communicates to us the Father's infinite mercy. On the lips of the catechist the first proclamation must ring out over and over: "Jesus Christ loves you; he gave his life to save you; and now he is living at your side every day to enlighten, strengthen and free you."[104]

The *kerygma* is the proclamation of the saving presence and action of the Trinitarian God in our lives, centred especially upon the Person of Jesus as the one who gave his life for us and is always present to us. The *kerygma* is focused, then, upon Jesus, but always Jesus *as Saviour through his paschal mystery* and always Jesus *in relation to the Spirit he sends and the Father* to whom he leads us. In its footnotes, the *Directory* points us to many Scriptural expressions of the *kerygma* as if to say, "There is not only one way of saying this. Be guided by making it about Jesus and his salvation in the context of the Persons of the Blessed Trinity".

---

[102] *DC* 57-60.

[103] We have already seen the importance of the place of the Blessed Virgin in appreciating the nature of evangelisation. Her role is also crucial with regard to the *kerygma* as well: in our translation of the "first proclamation" there are two Italian verbs that are used, almost interchangeably, not just in this *Directory* but in catechetical documents as a whole: *proclamare* and *annunciare*. "The first proclamation" might as easily be rendered "the first annunciation". The narrative of the Annunciation to Our Lady provides us with the prototype of the *kerygma* and the response of faith. It is no accident that the *Directory* is crowned with a consideration of Mary's place in paragraph 428. A *kerygma*tic catechesis is a Marian catechesis.

[104] *EG* 164.

The amount of space given to this consideration of the *kerygma* is a sign of the importance attached to it by the *Directory*. And yet this point about importance is not the main point to notice. In his encyclical on mission, *Redemptoris Missio*, Pope St John Paul II had already written, "Proclamation is the permanent priority of mission."[105] He had already committed the Church to be thinking of the annunciation of the central message of the Christian faith as the most pressing challenge in the work of evangelisation. What is new in this *Directory* is *the level of integration of the kerygma into the work of catechesis.* Catechesis, it says, should see itself also as a "proclamation" of the faith and should think that its task is now not only to deepen an already existent faith, but to help to generate that faith. Catechesis, then, should take this initial work of proclaiming the *kerygma* to itself and not only as a "first step", as it were, but as its *character*, as "the essential dimension of every moment of catechesis".[106]

What does this mean? The request that catechesis be understood as *kerygmatic* in character is central to the thrust of the catechetical renewal since before the Second Vatican Council. It is especially connected with the work of the Austrian Jesuit Johannes Hoffinger.[107] Those involved in his movement of renewal were concerned that in the work of ensuring in catechesis that the fullness of the faith was presented many were not grasping the unifying centre of the faith; they were losing the wood for the trees. The answer was to catechise always keeping a strong focus present, in every catechesis, on what the Scriptures call the "Mystery of Christ"[108]– that is, Christ's redemptive work within God's plan for us. In this way, the formation received in catechesis would always be integrated around the centre of the faith.

The *Directory*'s desire for catechesis to be *kerygmatic* is in part a pragmatic response to the fact that many ask for catechesis who have not yet heard or responded to the *kerygma*. Many come asking for a faith to be deepened when in fact the act of faith in Christ has yet to be made. But it is more than this. It is a recognition that the *kerygma* holds within itself the core of the faith, the central truths of the faith, and that catechesis can never move away from that centre without losing its way. All revealed truths flow from God and his plan; the Mystery of Christ is the deepest point of any truth that is taught, whether this is an aspect of the Creed, a petition of the Lord's prayer, a sacrament, or a requirement of justice. To find its rationale and motivating spring will always be to find that Mystery.

We have noted the *Directory*'s insistence that the *kerygma* is the *heart* of the Christian message. This is not the same thing as saying that it is the *first word* that is given by the catechist in any situation. We want to present clearly the very centre of

---

[105] St John Paul II, *Redemptoris Missio* (1990): 44.
[106] *DC* 57.
[107] Cf. for example, Johannes Hoffinger and Francis Buckley, *The Good News and its Proclamation* (Notre Dame, Indiana, University of Notre Dame Press, 1968).
[108] Cf. for example, *Romans* 16:25; *Ephesians* 3:4; *Colossians* 2:2, 4:3.

Christianity, but we know that there are pervasive cultural currents of thought that stand in our way – currents, for example, that see faith opposed to science, or that exalt the primacy of the individual will, seeing its unfettered use as the apex and goal of civilisation. These obstacles in terms of presuppositions or misunderstandings have to be cleared out of the way before the *kerygma* can be received or understood, for the *kerygma* presumes, among other things, a belief in God, a belief in the objectivity of truth, a belief in the order, meaningfulness and essential goodness of the universe. These are matters that we would call "preambles" to the faith. Many of those whom we are seeking to call to faith live with a worldview in which these dominate.[109] The catechist, as the *Directory* will note, needs to be aware of these currents in his or her own life and be formed so as to be able to address them so as to give people access to the life-giving truth of Christ.[110]

## THE CATECHUMENATE

The *Directory* moves next to a further major theme regarding the nature of catechesis, its "catechumenal" character. As it notes, this is a recovery that the Church is seeking of an ancient practice of receiving unbaptised converts into the Church. But the desire here is to do more than reinstate that process for the unbaptised (whether for children and adolescents or for adults). There is also a wish for this to be a source of inspiration for practising Catholics of any age who are already in full communion with the Church.[111] The catechumenate proper is described for us in outline in paragraph 63, detailing the stages of the *pre-catechumenate*, for accompaniment and proclamation of the *kerygma*; the *catechumenate* for a "comprehensive catechesis"[112] in the different dimensions of the Christian life; a period of *purification and enlightenment* for a more intense preparation for reception of the sacraments, and the final stage, known as *mystagogia*, the time after the reception of one or more of the sacraments of initiation which is a time for nurturing "an ever deeper experience of the mysteries of the faith and [by] incorporation into the life of the community."[113]

The paragraph following, no. 64, explains what it means in asking for the catechumenate to become a source of inspiration for catechesis as a whole. The points offered can act as criteria for assessing catechetical activity in different settings

---

[109] For example, cf. *DC* 355, 376-377. For an in-depth discussion of this cf. John Paul II's encyclical, *Fides et Ratio*, Faith and Reason, especially the section on what he calls the "indispensable requirements of the word of God" (80), those elements that need to be put in place for anyone to be able to *hear* what the herald has to say.

[110] Cf. *DC* 145.

[111] *DC* 62. So, for example, this request is followed through is the discussion on formation (135), in the section on the catechesis of children (242) and of adults (264) and discussing the co-ordination of catechesis in the diocese (421).

[112] *DC* 63.

[113] *DC* 63.

and the *Directory* requests that these be applied thoughtfully and carefully to help all catechesis take on this character in an appropriate way. The focus we are asked to take is on the person receiving catechesis and how he or she can be served best to receive all that the Church desires to give. The *Directory*, then, asks us to think of the importance of *continuity and progression* for a person, of providing an ongoing support in formation that is more than just episodic; it asks us to think of the importance of uniting the person with others in the enrichment of *community*, whether that is the parish, the family, the small group or the apostolate so that formation is not an isolating experience; we are to remember that our catechesis should be attractive and *address the whole person*, spirit, mind, emotions and body; that it should be ordered towards the *sacraments*, where Christ's grace is especially to be found; and that it should help people to "live the most intense moments...as *paschal events*" – to remember that we are baptised into Christ's death and resurrection and that this really *is* the pattern of our lives. In every event, and in every "death", small and great, he is united to us to bring us through that death into his life. Together, this helps us to see what can characterise catechesis as a whole, including the way we think of that ongoing formation in the faith after the sacraments of initiation have been received.[114]

## THE GOALS AND TASKS OF CATECHESIS

The attractive section of the *Directory* on the goals and tasks of catechesis follows the previous *Directory* closely.[115] The goals are expressed as enabling for a person a "living encounter with Christ",[116] with that sense of "encounter" that we have already discussed – not so much a single powerful experience so much as being in communion with him, coming to know Christ "ever better", developing a "mentality" which matches his "to the point of gradually coming to feel, think and act like Christ".[117] The *Directory* emphasises that this involves "the person in his totality", implies a "personal spiritual transformation" and the birth of the "new man".[118] The goal of catechesis is nothing less than the transformation of the person through his or her making Christ "the centre of the Christian life".[119]

The other point to notice in this section on the goals of catechesis is the reminder that when we find Christ and learn to live with him we necessarily find his Father and the Spirit. Jesus came to reveal the face of the Father and to bestow the Spirit for the fullness of life. The catechist is called to speak and teach simply about Jesus so that the centre of *his* life in the Blessed Trinity can emerge and those being catechised can

---

[114] *DC* 73-74.
[115] *GDC* 80-87.
[116] *DC* 75.
[117] *DC* 77.
[118] *DC* 76.
[119] *DC* 75.

understand his call to communion as a call to communion with the divine Persons of the Most Holy Trinity.[120]

The goal is communion with the divine Persons. The tasks express the way to that goal. The tasks can be matched to the four parts of the *Catechism*: knowledge and understanding of the faith, and especially the Creed (part 1); understanding the importance of participation in the celebration of the sacraments and liturgy (part 2); understanding the nature of the "good life of the Gospel", rooted in the promise of final and complete happiness with God, and expressed in the twofold commandment of love and the *Decalogue* (part 3); and learning the nature of prayer and the forms that prayer takes (part 4).

There is one further task, one further way to communion with the divine Persons, which the *Directory* wants to remind us about: learning a "spirituality of communion", of belonging to the Church.[121] The goal is heavenly communion and that heavenly life is learned and practised on earth through cultivating love for one's brother and sister in Christ. There is no other way than this. We can recall that the other four tasks of catechesis listed above are found in the New Testament in the very first description that we have of the Church, which goes on to speak of them having "all things in common".[122] In this final comment regarding the tasks of catechesis, then, the *Directory* returns us to the opening line of this chapter, that catechesis is an *ecclesial* act.[123]

---

[120] *DC* 78.
[121] *DC* 88-89.
[122] *Acts* 2:42-47.
[123] *DC* 55.

## THE SOURCES OF CATECHESIS

With this final section of the chapter[124] we move into the sphere of the holy. Catechesis, we remember is an echo of Christ and his teaching. What are the sources that convey that echo to us, down through the generations so that, in hearing and touching them, we hear and touch Christ? St John Paul, in his Letter introducing the *Catechism of the Catholic Church*, offered the new work as a point of renewal of catechesis and said that it could be this because it led the catechist and reader to "the living sources of the faith".[125]

All of the sources, the *Directory* tells us, are interrelated, as indeed they must be, for all have their unity in the one "Word of God, of which they are an expression".[126] Because of this unity and of their rootedness in the living Word each of them can be, the *Directory* teaches, "ways of catechesis". The catechist, then, can lead those being catechised along such ways, knowing that their source – and thus their destination – will be Christ himself. This confidence in the sources as ways of catechesis is supplemented by only a single caution – to practise a *balance* among the ways, according to the needs of the participants, so as not to offer a catechesis that is "one-dimensional", exclusively liturgical or biblical for example. To see what such a balance looks like, catechists have only to consult the index of citations in the *Catechism* itself, for the range and variety there.

A clarification is then offered concerning the phrase "Word of God". Whilst we use that phrase for the Sacred Scriptures because of their close connection with the Word, the *Directory* here means the eternal Word, the second person of the Blessed Trinity who reveals the Father and his plan, who lives eternally turned towards the Father as *his* source. That eternal Word is the one through whom creation came to be and is the principle of reason and order in the universe and in all history. In Jesus, we see that Word become flesh to be a gift poured out for every nation and, in his returning to the Father, bringing with him "the creation that he redeemed, which was created in him, and for him".[127]

All of the sources, the ways of catechesis, then, flow from and express that divine Word, which catechesis is to echo. In leading people along such paths, the catechist can help them encounter Christ, the source of each of them. And in so doing the catechist is stepping back and allowing Christ himself to be the point of reference, is facilitating the primary dialogue, which is not that of the catechist and the person being catechised, but rather concerns "the mystery of God who in Jesus enters into intimate dialogue with man".[128]

---

[124] This section is a much developed one from the 1971 *Directory* (a single paragraph, no.45), and the 1997 *Directory* (two paragraphs, nos. 95-96).
[125] *Fidei Depositum* (11th October 1992).
[126] DC 90.
[127] DC 91.
[128] DC 53.

The sources that express the Word are listed as *Sacred Scripture* (the "pre-eminent" source, which "reaches the depth of the human spirit better than any other word");[129] the *Magisterium*, the teaching office of the Church; the *liturgy*; the testimonies of the *saints and martyrs*, teaching us through their lives, their writings and their deaths; the prayerful reflection on the faith that we call *theology*; *Christian culture*, the ways of life that have been inspired by faith and have issued in a great intellectual, moral and artistic patrimony; and, finally, *beauty*, as a particular expression of goodness and truth. Catechesis, then, employs these sources, refers to them all of the time and *serves* them – the aim is always to put people in touch with them so that they may be led to Christ. For example, taking the case of the liturgy, the *Directory* teaches, "catechesis reaches its true fulfilment when the one being catechised takes part in the liturgical life of the community."[130] The liturgy is the source and summit of the Christian life and catechesis leads people to that place of encounter with Christ and source of his grace for their lives. Thus, we can see that the sources are not mere "tools" for catechesis, points for deriving elements for catechetical sessions. They are rather the channels and expressions of the Word with which one seeks to engage those being catechised.

Catechising with these sources is vital, then, since they give us access to those who knew the Lord *in the flesh*, to the One "we have seen with our eyes, which we have looked upon and touched with our hands...the word of life".[131] *The sources connect us to that original testimony*, to those who received his body and blood from his own hands, who were witnesses of the Resurrection, and whose lives and testimony, in word and in blood, stand as the foundation of the Church.[132] The *Scriptures* communicate and carry this witness to us, the *liturgy* takes us into the heart of Jesus's life, re-presenting the paschal mystery for us to share in it, the *Magisterium* takes us to the authoritative word of the apostles, commissioned by Christ to "teach all nations"[133], while the beginnings of the revolution that we call *Christian culture* reaches back to the Incarnation, to God who shared human life so that from that point on all people might share in his life. The apostles were also prominent among the original *saints and martyrs* and were also among the first *theologians* of the Church, those who reflected upon the Word which they knew and had touched.

While not listed as a separate source, it is worth noting that the lives and writings of *the Fathers of the Church* are also highlighted in a number of places, connected to various sources: "it is well that the life and works of the Fathers should find a suitable place among the contents of catechesis".[134] They are important, the *Directory* proposes,

---

129  *DC* 91
130  *DC* 96.
131  *1 John* 1:1.
132  *Revelation* 21:14.
133  *Matthew* 28:20.
134  *DC* 92.

because they show us the importance of the *Tradition* of the Church and the continuity between the first apostles and our own lives. Many were also confessors, *saints and martyrs* and their witness again helps us see the continuity between the earliest figures who gave their lives for Christ and our own time, linking us especially to the twentieth century "which has been called the *century of martyrdom*".[135] The Fathers are also vitally significant for appreciating how to catechise using our *theological* and *scriptural* sources, for they developed their theological reflections using a "sapiential approach",[136] seeking Christ as the wisdom of God and the living truth, with systematic reflection always united to the pursuit of divine wisdom. And their theology was in particular a reflection on the Scriptures, their writings beautiful tapestries of scriptural themes, images and allusions that witness to the unity of the Scriptures and the capacity of the sacred writings to illuminate contemporary challenges. The *Directory* also expressly mentions the Fathers in the section on the *liturgy*, highlighting the

---

[135]  *DC* 100. The *Directory* here may be thinking especially of the teaching of St John Paul II who, in his Apostolic Letter preparing for the Jubilee of the Year 2000, wrote, "The Church of the first millennium was born of the blood of the martyrs: *Sanguis martyrum – semen christianorum.* The historical events linked to the figure of Constantine the Great could never have ensured the development of the Church as it occurred during the first millennium if it had not been for the *seeds sown by the martyrs and the heritage of sanctity which marked the first Christian generations.* At the end of the second millennium, *the Church has once again become a Church of martyrs.*" (*Tertio Millennio Adveniente* 37).
[136]  *DC* 101.

importance of their "mystagogical catecheses", the presentations of the faith given to those who had received the sacraments of initiation and now needed to understand the implications of the sacraments for their lives.[137] It will be thinking of the catecheses of Fathers of the Church offered by figures such as St Augustine, St Ambrose and St Cyril of Jerusalem.

Scripture, Tradition and the Magisterium are listed first among the sources. The interdependence of these three has often been noted, as being something like a three-legged stool, providing balance and stability together. The Magisterium has the role of ensuring that the saving truth of Christ, "always the same and immutable",[138] which is handed down in writing (Sacred Scripture) and orally (Sacred Tradition), is always preserved and interpreted. The *Directory* reminds us that "the Roman pontiff and the bishops in communion with him are the custodians of the Magisterium of the Church."[139] A simple glance at the footnotes in the *Directory* confirms the importance of the Magisterium as a source, with papal teachings on the nature of catechesis and evangelisation being especially important.

The expanded section, from the earlier directories, on Christian culture as a source is crucially important for understanding catechesis today. The quotation from St Paul VI sums up the significance of this portion: the "split between the Gospel and culture is without a doubt the drama of our time".[140] The Christian faith unleashed a true revolution in the understanding of the human person and society.[141] David Bentley Hart puts it this way: "even Christianity's most implacable modern critics should be able to acknowledge that...we see something beginning to emerge from darkness into full visibility, arguably for the first time in our history: the human person as such, invested with the intrinsic and inviolable dignity, and possessed of an infinite value".[142] In Christianity we see "the creation of a new and original culture"[143] based on the vision of the human person as one who is created by God and "wonderfully restored and elevated in Christ".[144] This new and original culture has given rise to a vast intellectual, moral, social and aesthetic heritage wherever Christianity encountered another culture and it is urgent for catechists to make use of the expressions of Christian

---

137 *DC* 97.
138 *DC* 94.
139 *DC* 93.
140 *DC* 103, quoting Paul VI, *Evangelii Nuntiandi* (1975): 20.
141 The *Directory* lists, "the uniqueness of the human person, the dignity of life, freedom as a condition of human life, equality between men and women, the need to 'refuse the evil and choose the good' (Isaiah 7:15), the importance of compassion and solidarity, the significance of forgiveness and mercy and the necessity of being open to transcendence." (102)
142 *Atheist Delusions: The Christian Revolution and its Fashionable Enemies* (New Haven and London, Yale University Press, 2009) p.167.
143 *DC* 102.
144 *DC* 105, quoting Second Vatican Council, *Gaudium et Spes* (1965): 61.

culture in order to "educate believers, in a time of fragmentation, to the vision of the 'whole human person...'"[145] Catechists in many parts of the world now transmit the faith in a context of "cultural crisis" which has arisen from a rejection of the faith in the name of a "false concept of autonomy", the notion that the human person finds happiness only through the triumph of unfettered personal choice, irrespective of God, nature or morality. It is against this pervasive cultural position that catechesis must learn to speak, drawing on the witness of "the Christian vision of the world with the creative power of beauty".[146]

The explicit inclusion of *beauty* as a source is something new for the *Directory* to include, which now teaches that it is necessary for catechesis to follow the "way of beauty" (the *via pulchritudinis*) in all that is offered, "in order to reach the human heart".[147] This "way of beauty" was especially stressed by Pope Benedict XVI,[148] but is found earlier; for example in Pope St Paul VI who famously said, at the closing of the Second Vatican Council, "This world in which we live needs beauty in order not to sink into despair."[149] The thoughts in his *Letter to Artists* was in turn echoed by a similar Letter from St John Paul who appealed to artists, saying, "Beauty is a key to the mystery and a call to transcendence... the beauty of created things can never fully satisfy. It stirs that hidden nostalgia for God".[150] The emphasis on the importance of beauty, then, is not anything new in the history of the Church or in the teaching of the Magisterium, but *it has here been formally tied to the work of transmission of the faith*.

Some practical guidance and criteria for discernment of what is true beauty and not "apparently beautiful but empty, or even harmful, like the forbidden fruit in the earthly paradise (cf. *Genesis* 3:6)"[151] is also given. The criteria are found in the exhortation of St Paul: "whatever is true, whatever is honourable, whatever is just, whatever is pure, whatever is lovely, whatever is gracious, if there is any excellence, if there is anything worthy of praise, think about these things" (*Philippians* 4:8).[152] In the Christian tradition, as the *Directory* indicates,[153] beauty is always understood as the expression of unity, goodness and truth – the more perfect a being is, the more unity, truth, and goodness is present and, correspondingly, the more "radiance" or beauty. Thus, beauty is the

---

[145] *DC* 101.
[146] *DC* 105.
[147] *DC* 108.
[148] For a helpful set of articles, cf. D. Vincent Twomey SVD and Janet E. Rutherford (eds), *Benedict XVI and Beauty in Sacred Art and Architecture* (Dublin, Four Courts Press, 2011).
[149] St Paul VI, *Message to Artists* (1965).
[150] St John Paul II, *Letter to Artists* (1999): 16.
[151] *DC* 108.
[152] *DC* 108.
[153] *DC* 108.

*radiance* of unity, of goodness, and of truth.[154] The Christian tradition understands beauty to be the entry point to goodness, truth, and unity. In a world where there can be widespread resistance to the proclamation of truth, goodness and unity (so often it is only "my truth", "my view of the good", and "diversity" that are valued), the showing of beauty can reach the heart and capture it.

And here once again the interrelated nature of the sources of which the *Directory* writes can be seen clearly, for in this portion on beauty we are sent to the other sources to find beauty – to find beauty in the Scriptures, in the teaching of the Magisterium, in the liturgy, in Catholic culture, in the lives and testimony of the saints, and especially in the Blessed Virgin, the *tota pulchra* (the "all beautiful"). All of the sources are related because they all express Christ, "the fairest of the sons of men".[155]

## QUESTIONS FOR REFLECTION

1   Do I know the *kerygma*?
    • Can I express it simply, and in different situations?
    • Do I try to make my teaching *kerygmatic*, always linking the different topics I teach to the *kerygma*?

2   Do I ensure that in my Christian life I am fed from all of the sources for catechesis?
    • How far do I draw from each of them in my ministry?
    • Is there a balance there? Do I neglect any?

---

[154] According to St Thomas, for example, "unity" radiates as integrity, "goodness" radiates as proportion, and "truth" radiates as clarity (cf. *Summa Theologica* I, Q.39, a.8).
[155] *DC* 107, quoting Psalm 45:2.

# A Prayer for Catechists

HEAVENLY FATHER,

You sent your Son as the Good News for our lives.

May we learn to live in him and from him,

Wholly reliant on his gracious mercy,

And learn how to speak of him and his beauty to others.

We ask this in his name,

The name that is above all names,

Jesus Christ.

Amen.

CHAPTER III:

# The Catechist

The Preface and Introduction of the new *Directory* have already prepared us to find in this chapter a major focus of the whole text, for the quality of catechesis depends crucially upon *the person of the catechist*. As with the 1997 *Directory*, the discussion of the identity of the catechist in the Church takes place in the light of the *vocation of members of Christ's Body to different states in life*. In other words, the way in which lay people, religious and those who are ordained will act as catechists and evangelisers will flow directly from their vocation to the particular state in life to which God has called them. The particular responsibilities of the catechist and evangelist will vary according to the person's state in life, whether to the Sacrament of Holy Orders (bishop, priest and deacon), to consecrated religious life or to the lay vocation – those consecrated by their Baptism and Confirmation to engage in earthly affairs and "order them according to the plan of God".[156] The sections of this chapter, then, largely follow the different states of life and unpack how each is called to participate in the work of catechesis.

As we have seen, the *common* vocation of all of Christ's members in his Church – and thus of all catechists – is to holiness of life:

> Holiness is the crucial word that can be pronounced in presenting a new *Directory for Catechesis*. It is the herald of a way of life that catechists are also called to follow with constancy and fidelity.[157]

---

[156] Vatican Council II, *Lumen Gentium* 31. Within the lay vocation, the *Directory* gives special attention to the catechetical ministry asked of parents, of grandparents and of women and men.
[157] *DC*, Preface.

All catechists, therefore, in whatever state in life, are called to holiness as their primary vocation and the *Directory* rejoices in the fact that the Church, "in every part of the world, can present models of catechists who have attained holiness and even martyrdom in living their ministry every day." Flowing from this call to holiness, catechists are also called to *mission* for the sake of the evangelisation of the world. These two calls, to holiness and to mission, are common to all. The two are related to one another as breathing in and breathing out: coming close to Christ and his holiness is the necessary step for one to be able to be sent out by him to share in his mission.

Before moving into the details of how members of Christ's body serve as catechists in different states of life, the *Directory* has a significant introductory section placing the ministry of catechist *within the context of the whole Church* and presenting us with *the identity of the catechist in general*. Let us look at each in turn.

First, then, it is important to appreciate that there is a specific "ministry of catechesis"[158] within the Church. There is a specific vocation to be a catechist. Moreover, "only catechists who live out their ministry as a vocation can contribute to the efficacy of catechesis."[159] That is a strong statement, but it makes complete sense. Let us go back again to the final paragraph of the Preface to the *Directory*. Acknowledging the challenges of being a catechist, it calls on catechists to remember all of the great witnesses to catechesis over the Church's history and it concludes with a simple note of encouragement:

> Their witness is fruitful, and makes it still thinkable in our time that each of us can persevere in this adventure even in the silent, laborious, and sometimes thankless work of *being* a catechist.

The unadorned realism of the statement – with the unexpected but delightful invitation to see this vocation as an *adventure* – concludes with the emphasis on *being* a catechist. More important than what a catechist does is the sheer *being* of the catechist. The *Directory* will profile a range of aptitudes and skills for the catechist to gain and master. But the heart of this ministry lies in the spiritual realm, in the catechist's "yes" to this call from God to be at his service, to be docile to the Holy Spirit, to know that this is the *vocation* to which God has called one.

While there are many different ways in which one can receive this call to be a catechist – sometimes through the receiving of a sacrament, sometimes by a simple tap on the shoulder from the parish priest[160] – the important point is to realise that this is indeed a *specific vocation*. Only with that awareness will there be any sense of the *importance* of the ministry and the *need for formation* for this

---

[158] *DC* 110. Cf. also *CT* 13.
[159] *DC,* Preface.
[160] "They are all means which God, through the Church, uses to call people to his service". (*DC* 112)

calling.[161] And the *Directory* speaks to the importance of that sense of vocation and that need for formation for ordained, religious and lay people alike.[162]

Having identified this specific vocation to be a catechist, the *Directory* wishes to ensure that the catechist does not feel isolated from the Body of Christ's faithful. As we can recall, the opening of the *Directory* reminds us that catechesis is an *ecclesial* act, a ministry of the whole Church. It is the whole Christian community that is responsible for the ministry of catechesis – not that all are called to have that specific vocation (though many will have it – for example, all parents will) – but the community as a whole is like a mother, carrying and nurturing her new children in the faith, sustaining and supporting new members. It is striking how often the Church is described with this imagery of child-bearing,[163] as she gives rise to new members through the new life of faith and Baptism. Catechists know, then, that in their specific ministerial calling they can look to the wider community that is "the main provider of accompaniment in the faith".[164] The transmission of the faith to new members, and the deepening of faith in existing members, is a responsibility of all.

## THE IDENTITY OF THE CATECHIST

From this focus on the catechist having a specific identity and vocation within the Church, the *Directory* now moves on to explain what this identity is.[165] A rich and evocative description is given here of the catechist. It identifies *three pairs* of characteristics:

- A witness of faith and keeper of the memory of God
- A teacher and a mystagogue
- An accompanier and educator

---

[161]  The Preface to the *Directory* emphasises that "Quite a bit of attention has been dedicated to the theme of the formation of catechists, because it seems urgent to recover their ministry in the Christian community."

[162]  Cf. especially *DC* 151-156.

[163]  For example, the "bosom of the Church" (112), the "living womb of the Christian community" (131), "the womb in which for some of its members the specific vocation to the service of catechesis is born and grows" (133), "the womb of faith" (262). Again, it is worth noting the way in which the Blessed Virgin, as the one who received and carried Christ, is a type of the Church in this respect. The *Rite of Baptism* also carries this maternal imagery, of course. In *Catechesi Tradendae*, St John Paul II also uses this imagery of the ministry of catechesis, writing, "Catechesis aims therefore at developing understanding of the mystery of Christ in the light of God's word, so that the whole of a person's humanity is impregnated by that word." (*CT* 20)

[164]  *DC* 111.

[165]  It is worth noting the beautiful introductory sentence to this section, reminding us of this placing of the catechist within the broader context of the work of God and his Church: "By virtue of faith and baptismal anointing, in collaboration with the Magisterium of Christ and as a servant of the action of the Holy Spirit, the catechist is..." (*DC* 113).

Each of these characteristics is taken up in some depth in chapter four, when the *Directory* unpacks the implications for formation in each of these features. We will wait until we reach that section, therefore, to explore the precise meaning and importance of each of these. It is worth noting at this point, however, that the purpose of the pairing is to suggest the need for *three kinds of balance* in the life of the catechist.

The first point of balance is between the catechist as a personal, contemporary witness to the faith, living and speaking of the work of God in their own and others' lives, and the catechist as "keeper of the memory of God". The ability to be a witness speaks to the personal cost of being a catechist (in Greek, "witness" is *martus*, the word we use for "martyr" – and we have already seen that aspect of the catechist's calling highlighted in the Preface to the *Directory*). The catechist seeks, then, to *live* the faith that he or she proclaims and be able to give a personal *testimony* or *witness* to the faith. The *Directory* beautifully and sensitively addresses the inadequacy that all catechists feel when asked to provide a witness through their own lives: "Recognising his own frailty before the mercy of God, the catechist does not cease to be the sign of hope for his brothers". The testimony asked for is not to one's own perfection, or even to one's growth and maturity in the faith but, recognising one's own frailty, a testimony *to the Lord* and his patience, his abundant goodness and extravagant mercy, his evident healing and power.

The second member of this pair, "keeper of the memory of God", is a reminder to the catechist that the ministry belongs to God, just as he or she belongs to God. And so, while there needs to be an ability to offer a personal witness to the faith, just as important is the need to ensure that the ministry is seen to be rooted in faithfulness of God to the Church across all the ages. The catechist does not focus in any narrow way on his or her own life and testimony, but presents the whole of God's dealings with his people, his education of them. Joseph Ratzinger wrote of the need of the catechist to "live and think and speak out of the certainty of that larger memory in touch with the very depths of things."[166] As well as indicating a balance between these two aspects of being a catechist, there is also an inner connection between them, for in both cases one is witnessing to God and to his works, in the one case in the history of salvation, and in the other case in one's own experience and life.

The second balance asked of the catechist is between that of a *teacher* and a *mystagogue*. The first term is familiar enough. The catechist is not simply a facilitator of discussion or of the sharing of ideas, but one who is called upon to represent Christ the Teacher, who "utters the words of God" and who taught with authority.[167] The catechist is the teacher of what God has revealed and "Christ's spokesman, enabling

---

[166] Joseph Ratzinger, "Remarks made by Cardinal Ratzinger on the occasion of the *Catechism of the Catholic Church* at the Venerable English College in Rome on 27th May", *Briefing*, June 1994, p.4.
[167] *John* 3:34; *Matthew* 7:29.

Christ to teach with his lips."[168] *Mystagogue* is literally one who leads another "into the mystery." By "mystery" is meant the whole plan of God that was revealed in Christ and is now communicated to us in the sacred liturgy. That which we believe and teach is *given* to us in the sacraments of the Church. St Leo the Great wrote that "what was visible in our Saviour has passed over into his mysteries".[169] Christ's life and saving power are present and communicated to us in the sacraments, and especially of course in the Holy Eucharist, the Sacrament of sacraments. And so, as well as teaching Christ, the catechist leads people to him, to receive and share in his life. This pairing also, then, contains an inner connection between the two catechetical aspects. The catechist is being called to orientate his or her teaching to *point to* the liturgy and sacraments and also to *teach from* those same sacraments, explaining their meaning and the grace they give for one's life. Paragraph 98 provides a detailed account of what is entailed in the mystagogical aspect of the catechist's identity and ministry.

The third pair offered by the *Directory* is that the catechist is both an accompanier and an educator. Here, too, there is a point of balance being proposed together with an inner connection between these two qualities. The *Directory* speaks of expertise in both of these areas: the catechist is "an expert in the art of accompaniment" and "has educational expertise". The two dimensions complementing each other here might

---

[168] *CT* 6.
[169] St Leo the Great, *Sermo* 74, 2:PL 54, 398.

be thought of as *providing support* on the one hand, and assisting the person to *take responsibility for their own learning* on the other. It is a pair of attributes centred very much on relational skills and attitudes.

The first quality, that of *accompaniment*, focuses our attention on the importance of the personal, one-to-one attentiveness the catechist gives to the one being catechised. If we return briefly to the narrative of the annunciation, one of the striking points we can notice is how *particular and detailed* is the description of where Gabriel is to go and to whom he is to give his message: "…to a city of Galilee named Nazareth, to a virgin betrothed to a man whose name was Joseph, of the house of David; and the virgin's name was Mary."[170] God knows the one to whom he sends his catechist. His sending is intentional, focused and personal. Knowing this, the catechist can confidently commit to accompanying the person, providing stability and continuity for the one being catechised, knowing that God's plan will unfold for the person over time.

The term "accompaniment" carries with it both the sense of a *journey* and *staying with the person on that journey*. And this is not to be confused with an aimless wandering, without a destination clearly in mind. The idea is rather that of travelling together on the Way that is Christ. The *Directory* explains it as helping another to "mature in the Christian life and journey towards God".[171] As we have seen, the first name for Christians was that of "followers of the Way", and that Way was well-defined from the outset: we find it already set out in *Acts* 2:42 as the following of the apostles' teaching, the prayers, the breaking of the bread and life together (i.e. the four dimensions that we have already seen as the tasks of catechesis that lead us to the goal of communion with Christ).

We can gain further insight into the meaning of accompaniment by noting that it is etymologically linked to the word "companion" and so the catechist as accompanier is one who will be a companion to someone on the "pilgrimage" of faith. That word in turn is derived from the Latin "cum" and "pan", "with bread", and this is helpful for thinking about a link to another quality of the catechist that we have already mentioned, that of being a mystagogue. The mystagogue, we remember, is the one who leads the person into the mystery of Christ, and especially to where Christ is to be encountered in the sacraments, centred on the Eucharist. This is where the catechist as accompanier and mystagogue leads the person to find the true and living Bread for the journey. It is where both catechist and the one being catechised find their nourishment together.

The second member of this pair is that of *educator*. The term indicates someone who is concerned with training and formation. To that extent it is a broader concept than teacher since it implies an interest in the development of the whole person – taking into account their spiritual life, their intellect, emotions, and their physical and

---

[170] *Luke* 1:26.
[171] *DC* 113c.

psychological well-being. The educator is concerned with what the *Directory* calls an "integral formation" of the person in this broad sense.[172] What we gain from this pair of attributes, then, is a sense of the catechist being concerned about the development and well-being of the whole person in an ongoing way.

The *Directory*'s vision of catechists as possessing these six qualities is certainly a challenging one for individual catechists and also for the institutions and settings in which they are formed. It is probably true to say that the majority of catechists do not as yet have a good understanding of either the significance and nobility of their vocation nor of what the Church is asking of them. It will be important, then, to see how these themes are picked up in the next chapter, on the formation of catechists, to understand how the Church would like to support her catechists to gain this kind of spirituality, these perspectives, attitudes and skills. Before moving on to that, however, we can turn to the *Directory*'s presentation on the identity of catechists according to their state in life.

## THE BISHOP, THE PRIEST AND THE DEACON AS CATECHISTS

Everything which the *Directory* has presented so far in terms of the identity of the catechist is supremely the case for the bishop since he is the "first",[173] the pre-eminent catechist. It is therefore appropriate that the Preface presented a bishop of the Church, St Turibius, as the patron of the *Directory* and as a model for catechists and evangelisers. St Turibius's work as a catechist flowed from his episcopal consecration: "He understood his episcopal ministry as evangeliser and catechist." Thus, for example, he "acted as a catechist by producing in Spanish, Quéchua, and Aymara the first catechisms for the indigenous people of South America."[174]

Priests are "co-workers" with the bishop in catechesis, while deacons exercise a specific "*diakonia*" to the Word of God.[175] What is clear about how the *Directory* sees all of those possessing the sacrament of Orders is that each is *personally* called to embrace the vocation of catechist as one significant aspect of their sacramental calling. Each will live out that role of the catechist slightly differently, according to the nature of their particular office, and their personal – rather than delegated – involvement in catechesis is the first point of emphasis in the *Directory*. Thus, for example, the bishop will "concern himself with catechesis by engaging directly in the transmission of the Gospel and keeping the deposit of faith intact";[176] priests

---

[172] *DC* 135b.

[173] "First" here, "primo" in Italian, carries the sense of "the most important" and also the "first in order", the source of the authority of other catechists.

[174] *DC*, Preface.

[175] *DC* 115, 117. "*Diakonia*", from which we derive the word "deacon" is from the Greek "*diakonos*", meaning "servant".

[176] *DC* 114a.

will both dedicate themselves "with competent and generous commitment to the catechesis of the faithful entrusted to their pastoral care" and also act as the "catechist of catechists, taking care of their formation";[177] while deacons are particularly to "proclaim the word in their professional lives" in addition to the homilies they give.[178]

In addition to their personal involvement in catechesis, those having the sacrament of Orders all have responsibilities for the *organisation, planning and formation aspects of others who are involved in catechesis*. The bishop obviously has the greatest overall responsibility for the work of catechesis, ensuring at the diocesan level that there is a plan for catechesis in the diocese, that it is well-resourced and that catechists are effectively formed and supported by high quality resources. Priests, his co-workers, carry out these functions and this oversight at the parish level. There is a particular focus in this section regarding priests on a commitment to identifying, valuing and forming catechists, giving his "utmost concern to this task" and seeing them as a valuable mature group in the parish who can be co-responsible with him in the area of general parish formation.[179] Deacons who are married are asked to have a

---

[177] *DC* 116 a, f.
[178] *DC* 117.
[179] *DC* 116.

particular focus on the catechesis and support of families and also ensure that all those who could slip out of the parish's vision and be neglected in her catechetical work – the elderly and the sick, for example – are provided with good catechesis and integrated into the life and catechetical mission of the parish.[180]

Two other points are worth briefly noting before we move on. First, that the link between catechesis and the liturgy is again highlighted in this section. The deacon is one who unites liturgy, catechesis and the life of charity in his own person. The priest "takes care" of those same links, while the bishop "should feel the urgency, at least during the more intense periods of the liturgical year, particularly during Lent, to call the people of God to the cathedral in order to catechise them."[181]

The second point is to note that, in addition to Canon Law and relevant directories for those in Orders, the *Directory* points us to St John Paul II's words to bishops and priests to source this section. The saint's words express an intensity and passion about catechesis that the *Directory* surely wants us to experience in order to appreciate the Church's conviction about the vital importance of the catechetical role of those in Orders. To bishops, St John Paul II wrote:

> I know that your ministry as Bishops is growing daily more complex and overwhelming. A thousand duties call you: from the training of new priests to being actively present within the lay communities, from the living, worthy celebration of the sacraments and acts of worship to concern for human advancement and the defense of human rights. But let the concern to foster active and effective catechesis yield to no other care whatever in any way. This concern will lead you to transmit personally to your faithful the doctrine of life. But it should also lead you to take on in your diocese, in accordance with the plans of the episcopal conference to which you belong, the chief management of catechesis, while at the same time surrounding yourselves with competent and trustworthy assistants. Your principal role will be to bring about and maintain in your Churches a real passion for catechesis, a passion embodied in a pertinent and effective organisation, putting into operation the necessary personnel, means and equipment, and also financial resources. You can be sure that if catechesis is done well in your local Churches, everything else will be easier to do. And needless to say, although your zeal must sometimes impose upon you the thankless task of denouncing deviations and correcting errors, it will much more often win for you the joy and consolation of seeing your Churches flourishing because catechesis is given in them as the Lord wishes.[182]

Of the catechetical ministry of priests, he said:

---

[180] *DC* 118.
[181] *DC* 114.
[182] *CT* 63.

Today, the boundaries of the priest's ministry are increasingly being extended to include pastoral contexts that enrich the Christian community but sometimes risk fragmenting his activity into thousands of commitments and activities. His attention to catechesis suffers from this as it can be reduced to sporadic moments that have little effect on the formation of catechists. After the example of the Apostle Paul (cf. *Romans* 1: 14), he must instead feel, as it were, indebted to the entire people of God to preach the Gospel and to do so with the most careful theological and cultural preparation. The *General Directory for Catechesis* notes: "Experience bears out that the quality of catechesis in a community depends very largely on the presence and activity of the priest" (n. 225). As the first catechist in the community, the priest, especially if he is a parish priest, is called to be the first believer and disciple of the Word of God, and to devote painstaking care to the discernment and guidance of vocations to catechetical service. As a "catechist of catechists" he must be concerned with spiritual, doctrinal and cultural formation.[183]

## CONSECRATED PERSONS AS CATECHISTS

The section on consecrated persons and catechesis is very short, but makes significant points. We should not miss the powerful statement that their specific contribution cannot be replaced by either priests or laity. Those living a consecrated life as religious carry the all-important character of *witness* wherever they go, simply because of the vows they take and way of life they embrace, which speaks the "eloquent language of a transfigured life".[184] We are already familiar with the importance which the *Directory* attaches to the concept of witness as giving credibility and coherence to the proclamation of the Gospel.

In the next paragraph the *Directory* speaks of the immense work in the area of catechesis that different communities have carried out, each with their individual charisms. One thinks of the Dominicans and Franciscans, the Benedictines and Salesians, the numerous orders of sisters who have been dedicated to parish and school education and to ministry and catechesis for families. Often it has been religious who have accompanied immigrants, helping them to establish systems of catechesis in new cultures and settings. It is not an insignificant point that the *Directory* "awaits with hope a renewed commitment to the service of catechesis",[185] for there was an exodus from this area of ministry in the years following the Second Vatican Council, leaving a challenging gap for the Church regarding the adequate formation of lay people to enter into this field.

---

[183] St John Paul II, *Address to the Participants in the Convention 'The Clergy and Catechesis in Europe'* (8th May 2003): 2-3.
[184] *DC* 119.
[185] *DC* 120.

## LAY CATECHISTS

The final section in this chapter treats of the role of lay people as catechists. There is an introduction to this theme followed by a discussion of the role of parents and grandparents and then of women and men. There are several noteworthy points about this presentation. First, this is the first time that grandparents have been accorded a particular place in a directory for catechesis. Secondly, this is also the first time that there has been a specific discussion of the role of women in catechesis. As we will see, men are not neglected in this section, but it is the role of women that the *Directory* wished to highlight. Finally, the decision has been made to place the discussion of parents as catechists within the umbrella of "lay catechists" rather than to address the two groups separately. We will try to understand why this is the case.

We begin, then, with the general points made about lay catechists. These introductory paragraphs distinguish the lay vocation, grounded in the sacraments of Baptism and Confirmation, to restore the secular world to Christ, from the specific vocation to be a catechist. The former is a vocation to serve Christ in the world; the latter to serve him in the members of his body through their work of formation. The former takes place mainly through the life and witness of the lay person ("their very life as disciples is a form of proclamation of the Gospel"),[186] while the latter involves "a more organic and structured catechesis".[187] Within the specific vocation to serve as a catechist in the Church the *Directory*, quoting from its 1997 predecessor, then distinguishes between two broad groups: on the one hand the main volunteer and part-time catechists who make up the majority of lay people serving in this ministry, and on the other a smaller number of "publicly recognised and permanently dedicated"[188] lay people who serve in the diocese to assist the bishop.

The introductory comments about the lay vocation in general do not have the status merely of a preamble which is irrelevant to the main considerations. The point to realise is that, as with the ordained ministry and with consecrated persons, the *lay character* has an influence on how the identity of the catechist is lived out. That lay identity also affects considerations of how lay catechists are formed and the particular responsibilities they have in catechesis.[189]

Only a single paragraph[190] is given to the role of *parents* in catechesis and interestingly, the focus here is mainly on one point: that parents have the responsibility

---

[186] *DC* 121.

[187] *DC* 122.

[188] *DC* 123.

[189] Thus, St John Paul II wrote that: "the lay faithful must be formed according to the *union* which exists from their being *members of the Church and citizens of human society.*" *Christifideles Laici* (1988): 59. Lay formation, in other words, must respect the particular lay character and the mission of lay people to transform society.

[190] *DC* 124.

to be the "first catechists of their own children" and that this role should not be taken away from them through mistaken attitudes or by default through the way in which catechesis is organised in a parish or school. That parents are the pre-eminent catechists of their children is a well-rehearsed point, restated over and again in Church documents, encyclical letters, in the *Catechism* and so on.[191] The *Directory* just makes a single point in this regard: that the catechetical role of parents is grounded in the sacrament of matrimony – in other words, that it flows from their vocation to marriage. Catechesis is an aspect of a couples' *vocation* and not a task which may or may not be taken up. The *Directory* at this point might have quoted from St John Paul II:

> The task of giving education is rooted in the primary vocation of married couples to participate in God's creative activity: by begetting in love and for love a new person who has within himself or herself the vocation to growth and development, parents by that very fact take on the task of helping that person effectively to live a fully human life.[192]

All of this, then, is taken for granted in this paragraph which wants to pin-point why in practice this role is not more easily or commonly exercised and why it is not, perhaps, always taken seriously by parents themselves. The *Directory* locates the difficulty first of all in "the mentality of delegation that is so common", with parents giving way to "specialists in religious education". A false form of professionalism in catechetics has made parents question their own capacity to hand on the faith in the home. Coupled with this the *Directory* points to practices in the Christian community (here, especially the parish) that can inadvertently exclude parents from catechetical offerings as it struggles "to organise family centred catechesis which starts from the families themselves". The *Directory* here, then, issues a powerful challenge to the Church to find ways to assist parents "in the fulfilment of their educational mission". Having seen the content of this paragraph, it is easier to understand the decision to place the role of parents *within* the section on lay catechists as a whole rather than treat of parents in a separate section: the *Directory* precisely wants to overcome this separation between "catechists" and "parents" that continues to hobble the Church's catechetical work.

The catechetical and pastoral realism which characterises the discussion about parents is very evident also in the paragraph following which is concerned with *godparents and sponsors*.[193] Clearly, if parents are to take up their role as catechists of

---

[191] For example, in the *Catechism* we read, as it gathers a number of Church sources, "'The role of parents in education is of such importance that it is almost impossible to provide an adequate substitute.' (*GE* 3) The right and the duty of parents to educate their children are primordial and inalienable (cf. *FC* 36)." (*CCC* 2221)
[192] *FC* 36.
[193] *DC* 125.

their children, one of the pastoral avenues for assisting them is for the Church to take seriously the role of godparents and sponsors, those who have specific responsibility for helping parents in their role. The *Directory* has three concrete proposals to make here: first of all, to assist parents in the process of *selection*, especially in the light of the objective criteria required by the Church.[194] Secondly, to offer some formation for godparents "which may help them to rediscover the gift of faith and of belonging to the Church". And finally, to have figures from the local Christian community who can take this role "as witnesses of faith and ecclesial presence".

A second, very realistic and helpful way in which the *Directory* highlights the need to give assistance to parents to support a focus on family catechesis is by speaking of the importance of *grandparents*.[195] The *Directory* recognises the increased importance of grandparents "in the face of family crisis" – in many ways grandparents not only support parents but even substitute for them in difficult periods. At the same time, there is a broader theme being brought into play here: that the three-generation family is a naturally healthy and supportive structure for the raising of children in the faith, with grandparents being a "great treasure" in many ways, spiritual and religious and also social and relational. There is a particular relationship that grandparents have

---

[194] "...the choice of godparents...not motivated by faith but based on family or social customs... has contributed in no small way to the degradation of these educational figures." (*DC* 125) For the objective criteria, the *Directory* refers us to the *Code of Canon Law* (canon 874) and the *Eastern Code of Canon Law* (canon 685).
[195] *DC* 126.

to children that is unique to them and it often includes more time and an ability to listen and encourage as well as pass on their experience of the faith. Children can see in grandparents the way in which faith is transmitted from generation to generation, with the continuity of the faith enfleshed in their own family.

The final section of this treatment of lay catechists is dedicated to the theme of women in catechesis. It is again a sign of the realism of the *Directory* that this occasions and merits a specific discussion for it is a fact that women make up the majority of lay catechists – the *Directory* speaks of the "great contribution offered by female catechists".[196] This is not simply a numerically superior contribution, however, for the *Directory* tries to identify some of the qualities that characterise the "genius of women" in this vocation. "Genius" here, as in other Church documents, means the innate spirit, or character, that which marks out the specific contribution that a person or group makes. The "genius" of women, then, is the identification of what it is that women specifically bring to the vocation of catechesis by virtue of their being women. And this is something that the *Directory* immediately says is "essential and indispensable".

The *Directory* ties this genius to the capacity for *motherhood.* Women have in Mary the model they can look to of maternal love,[197] and we have already seen that the image of maternity is a recurring image used for all catechetical work in the Church: the bearing of the Word until it becomes mature in one's life and is the source of new life for others as well as for oneself. Because Our Lady is also the type of the Church, the genius of women, the *Directory* points out, is especially helpful in "knowing how to bear witness, even in difficult moments, to the tenderness and devotion of the Church".[198] This reflection also suggests that the involvement of women in catechesis also means that a particular charism of *care* is often brought to bear, both with regard to people and to things. While this treatment is not intended to be exhaustive, it is trying to suggest ways in which the general identity of the catechist is expressed in a particular way through the ministry of women.

The final paragraph concludes by speaking briefly of men as catechists, and the *Directory* here stresses that in devoting space to the contribution of women it does not intend to overshadow the "equally significant" presence of men. The particular masculine "genius" is not explored here, but the importance of the fatherly role has already been emphasised by the Church.[199] The *Directory* does go on to indicate the current challenging cultural situation in which male and female are often viewed as mere social constructs and are placed at the mercy of the human will which imagines

---

[196] *DC* 128.
[197] *DC* 127.
[198] *DC* 127.
[199] Cf. for example, St John Paul II, *Familiaris Consortio* (1981): 25; *Homily to the Faithful of Terni* (19th March 1981): 3-5: *AAS* 73 (1981), 268-271.

that it can ignore the reality or significance of sexual differences and override or reconstruct sexual identity. In this situation, it is "indispensable" that both men and women are involved in the catechetical ministry, witnessing to the need for both sexes to be involved in Christian formation and growth. And this point is not presented as a mere reaction to the "signs of the times". Rather, it is offered as a perennial truth that "for healthy human and spiritual growth one cannot do without both presences, female and male".

## QUESTIONS FOR REFLECTION

1   Looking at the different qualities of a catechist (teacher, educator, mystagogue, accompanier, witness and keeper of the memory of God) how do I think of myself at this moment in relation to each of them?
    • How far do I see myself undertaking each of these roles in my ministry?
    • How is each of them expressed in my work of catechesis currently?
2   In which of the roles would I like to be further formed?

# A Prayer for Catechists

HEAVENLY FATHER,
You have made us your children in Christ.
Our true identity is that we are your sons and daughters,
Precious to you,
Members of your family,
Made in your image
And being restored day by day to your likeness
   through your grace.
May we live always from the truth of this identity
And know ourselves as we are in your eyes.
We ask this in the name of the One who came
   to bestow on us your gaze of everlasting love,
Your Son and our Lord, Jesus Christ.
Amen.

# CHAPTER IV:

# Formation of the Catechist

When thinking about the formation of catechists, it is easy to make the first question we need to answer, "*Where* shall we send the catechists for their formation?" That question of "Where?" is indeed asked in this chapter, but it is in fact one of the final points to be considered. The *initial* question asked by the *Directory* is, "*Who* will form the catechist?"

## WHO FORMS CATECHISTS?

In the opening section of this chapter, that question and its answer is given a historical context: "Who formed the *first* catechists and disciples?" We know the answer: it was *Christ*. "At the beginning of Christianity, formation, which was lived in experiential form, revolved around the vital encounter with Jesus Christ".[200] What did this "experiential form" look like? Jesus called his disciples and they stayed with him for a number of years. He taught them, prayed with them, spoke with them. They were able to observe how to related to others, healing and teaching, responding to opponents, and calling to faith. It is Christ who formed his first disciples, who then became his witnesses. Introducing others to Christ is the *goal* of catechesis and so knowing him must also be the *source* of formation. As a catechist one leads others to the person by whom one has already been found. For catechists today, we also are called to "stay" with Christ in prayer, in the sacraments, through our reading of the Scriptures and through

---

[200] *DC* 130.

studying the teaching of the Church. In these ways, we also can be gradually formed by him, day by day.

Formation, therefore, is Christ-centred: it is primarily a matter of being conformed to Christ, internalising his message and being "profoundly touched" by him, allowing his Spirit to mould one's heart. This is a process, the *Directory* rightly says, that takes place "deep within the catechist".[201] The formation of the catechist is primarily a *spiritual formation* undertaken by Christ and his Spirit in the "womb" of the Church.[202]

The next point flows from this: *Christ's disciples were formed to be with him on his mission.* Throughout the time that Christ was with his disciples on earth he was forming them so that they in turn could go out, and "go ahead" of him, preparing for him. Today's formation, also, is to have this character, to make catechists aware that "as baptised persons they are true *missionary disciples*".[203] St Luke gives us an account of Jesus first sending out the twelve, who then return and tell Jesus what they have done.[204] A second sending follows, this time of seventy (or seventy-two) disciples, who are sent out two by two into "every place where he himself was about to come".[205] This second group anticipates the universal mission of the Church that will be launched at Pentecost.[206] The catechists are formed to participate in this work of evangelisation, with the special focus of assisting believers in their ongoing growth in faith.

The text then moves onto a further connected point in a short section called "The Christian community as privileged place of formation".[207] Christ gathered a community of disciples around him to carry out his work. He does not separate himself from his disciples. Catholic doctrine speaks of this truth using the phrase *Christus totus*, meaning the *whole*, or complete, Christ. Christ has so closely united himself to his disciples, to the Church, that *together* they make up "one Christ". As St Augustine taught:

> Let us rejoice then and give thanks that we have become not only Christians, but Christ himself. Do you understand and grasp, brethren, God's grace toward us? Marvel and rejoice: we have become Christ. For if he is the head, we are the

---

[201] *DC* 131.

[202] *DC* 131.

[203] *DC* 132.

[204] *Luke* 9:1-6, 10.

[205] *Luke* 10:1-12, 17-20.

[206] The number of disciples here is a biblical reference to the number of the nations of the world. For the same reason, the translation of the Old Testament into Greek is called the "Septuagint" following the tradition that it was undertaken by seventy scholars in order to enable God's Revelation to reach all of the nations. For a brief discussion cf. Benedict XVI, *Jesus of Nazareth, From the Baptism in the Jordan to the Transfiguration* (London, Bloomsbury Publishing, 2007) pp. 179-180.

[207] *DC* 133-134.

members; he and we together are the whole man...the fullness of Christ then is the head and the members. But what does "head and members" mean? Christ and the Church.[208]

When the *Directory* writes of the encounter with Christ, or formation by Christ, it intends us to think always of Christ, head and members, Jesus together with his people.

Precisely because of that doctrine the *Directory* states that the formation of its catechists should be above all the work of Christ united to, and working in the local Church, in the community of real people who know and live around the catechists. Yes, this community will have its weaknesses and limitations, just as that initial group of Christ's disciples did, and objectively speaking there might be a group or place far away who would do a better job at formation, but in the end a catechist needs to be able to learn from those followers of the Lord who are close by so that they can be accompanied and formed over an extended period by those who live and bear witness to the faith "in a natural way". John Paul had asked for this local parish-based training in *Catechesi Tradendae*:

> ...every big parish or every group of parishes with small numbers has the serious duty to train people completely dedicated to providing catechetical leadership.[209]

As we will see later in the chapter, this desire for locally-based formation, together with that sense of "naturalness" that can be present in such local formation, is not implying that there should either be an absence of formal study undertaken together, nor the exclusion of more structured external support for formation. But we do see an emphasis being placed on the local and the proximate for the carrying of ongoing formation.

This seems an attractive picture to paint, for the local parish to be responsible for its own work of formation, with all of the advantages of personal accompaniment that go with this; nevertheless, we might ask: is it not unrealistic to expect sound, orthodox and comprehensive formation to flow from such an approach? In fact, the *Directory* is very well aware of challenges in such an approach, and of the disastrous situation that could follow from poorly formed members of the local parish trying to assist others. As we shall see, then, the *Directory* proposes that, in the first place, *priests* should be formed to a point of *catechetical excellence* in order to lead this formation[210] and that, together with the priest, there should be a *group of catechists* who are formed to maturity together. The aim, therefore, in a parish, is for a priest to have the assistance of a group of well-formed catechists who engage in ongoing, local formation of others together.

---

[208] *In ev Jo.* 21, 8: PL 35, 1568, cited in *CCC* 795.
[209] *CT* 67.
[210] Cf. *DC* 151-153.

## CRITERIA OF FORMATION

Having considered the question of *"who* forms?", the substantial portion of the rest of this chapter is dedicated to the question of *how* the formation takes place and what the *content* is of this formation. The main thing to bear in mind when reading this section of the chapter is that *everything* in formation is to serve its *goal*: that of the catechist being more and more closely conformed to Christ, who leads us to the Father in the Holy Spirit, so that the catechist can in turn help others towards that goal. Every element of formation – how it is undertaken and what is presented and taught – is for the sake of that goal of the catechist knowing and loving Christ and helping others to find and be formed in him as well.

The *Directory* provides us with six *criteria for formation*; in other words, *how* it needs to take place. One of these criteria the *Directory* repeats from its predecessor:

> As a general criterion, it is necessary to underline the need for a coherence between the general pedagogy of formation of catechists and the pedagogy proper to the catechetical process. It would be very difficult for the catechist in his activity to improvise a style and a sensibility to which he had not been introduced during his own formation.[211]

This makes a lot of sense: *form catechists in the way that they themselves will form others*. Catechists can hand on only what they have learned, and they will hand on the truths of the faith in *the way* they have learned. Thus, if the formation of the catechist is only superficially based on Christ, that will be the character of their own formation of others. If a catechist is not formed to rely on the Holy Spirit, he or she will not teach others to live in this way. The criteria offered here, therefore – for the formation of every priest and catechist, every parish volunteer, parent, teacher and diocesan leader, as well as for every apostolate that assists in formation – are the necessary elements that need to *characterise the formation offered*, that need to provide its "style", so that those formed in this way will be able to communicate it to others in their turn.

The list of criteria begins with a reminder about the identity of the catechist. When involved in the formation of others we need to remember that we are assisting in the formation of persons who *receive* their being from God and are being asked by God to *make a gift* of their lives to others. Those responsible for formation are helping a person learn how to (spiritually) breathe in and breathe out, to *receive* from God in order to in turn be generous in *giving him or herself* to others.

The risk in formation if we fail to do this is what the *Directory* describes as either "self-absorption" and the "collapse of fervour" or else "a sterile pastoral over-exertion".[212] In other words, either too much self-concern, with catechists overly-interested in their own performance as catechists, or else trying to offer themselves

---

[211] *DC* 135d.
[212] *DC* 135a.

for ministry in ways that end in burnout. In this latter case, one gives of oneself, exerts oneself on behalf of others, but can become disenchanted with the vocation because of a sense of lack of response from others, or else a lack of stable convictions about the importance of what one is doing. It becomes more and more "my" work and less and less something to which I am being obediently responsive *because of Christ's call to me*, the experience of a love which I am seeking to share. The twin dangers of self-protection and pastoral overreach are not new. In the thirteenth century, St Bernard of Clairvaux said it in this way:

> Today there are many in the Church who act like canals, the reservoirs are far too rare. So urgent is the charity of those through whom the streams of heavenly doctrine flow to us, that they want to pour it forth before they have been filled; they are more ready to speak than to listen, impatient to teach what they have not grasped, and full of presumption to govern others while they know not how to govern themselves.
>
> You too must learn to await this fullness before pouring out your gifts, do not try to be more generous than God. The reservoir resembles the fountain that runs to form a stream or spreads to form a pool only when its own waters are brimming over. The reservoir is not ashamed to be no more lavish than the spring that fills it.[213]

---

[213]  St Bernard of Clairvaux, *Sermon 18, On the Song of Songs.*

The *Directory*, with St Bernard, counsels helping the person in formation learn how to live from the Source, returning to it constantly, so as to be formed in self-gift and mission by "starting out ever anew" from one's union with God.

The *Directory* continues its counsels of care for those being formed with a very simple, but important, reminder to always keep in mind the tasks which the catechist will need to undertake – leading others to the knowledge of the faith, initiating them into the celebration of the Mystery, forming them for life in Christ, teaching prayer and leading them to share more deeply in the life of the local church. We have already seen that the catechist will need to be able to transmit "not only a teaching but also an integral Christian formation" and is being asked by the Church to use the catechumenal model of formation in stages, uniting the pastoral, liturgical and catechetical dimensions. In that case, then, this kind of 'integral Christian formation" is what needs to characterise the catechist's own formation.[214]

It then highlights the pastoral aspect of formation: "the Church feels the duty of forming its catechists in the art of personal accompaniment",[215] and draws the simple conclusion of the kind which we have already seen – since catechists are being asked to accompany others they must be given "the experience of being accompanied in order to grow in discipleship". Catechists in formation must know from experience what it is to have someone who not only teaches them, but stays with them, takes an interest in their own spiritual life, their struggles to commit, their questions and difficulties, and assists them in their growth in trusting the Lord and his Church. The *Directory* is aware that this is the crying need in the Church and that catechists are so often left without any help or guidance of any kind and that this aspect of formation is crucial to put in place.

This kind of accompaniment is focused especially on two attitudes that the formator, or mentor figure, is trying to build in the one being formed. The first is *"an attitude of docibilias and of self-formation"*.[216] This attitude is really one of those "pairs" of attributes beloved by the authors of the *Directory*. *Docibilias* means an aptness for being taught. One is helping the person being formed to be *teachable*. A teacher or formator can only do so much. In the end, it is the attitude of the person being taught that is the key: does one *want* to learn or is one resistant through pride or self-doubt or laziness? No one can *make* another person understand, or come to faith. St Augustine reminds us of the limitations facing the catechist: "a person beholding these truths in the present life...cannot make his hearer also see them if such a one is hindered by defilement of heart."[217] Being teachable is therefore a *virtue* which must be strenuously

---

[214] *DC* 135b.
[215] *DC* 135c.
[216] *DC* 135e.
[217] St Augustine, *De fide et symbolo*, 9, 20, in R.P. Russell, O.S.A. (trans.). *Faith and the Creed* (New York, Fathers of the Church, Inc., 1955).

practised. G.K. Chesterton once wrote about "contentment" that it is something one has to work at: "True contentment is a thing as active as agriculture. It is the power of getting out of any situation all that there is in it. It is arduous and it is rare".[218]

*Docibilias* is a similarly arduous work. It is a matter of facing honestly one's *resistance* to learning, one's acceptance of sloppy thinking, of living by platitudes, of avoiding the challenging truths in the faith that would demand change in one's life. Above all it entails acknowledging one's struggle with trust and obedience. The *Directory* paints the picture of the person who has *docibilias*, having "the willingness to be touched by grace, by life, by persons in a serene and positive attitude toward reality in order to *learn how to learn*."[219]

*Self-formation* is the other member of this pair. One is trying to assist catechists to have the ability to "look after and nourish" the life of faith "independently".[220] This is the style of formation, in other words, that consists in helping teach a person how to fish rather than giving him fish. In the fifth century St Augustine emphasised the importance of this kind of teaching to fish in matters of the faith. He compared two ways of teaching: the first, he says, is like reading to others; the second is teaching a person how to read. It is this second way that we need to practise in matters of the faith.[221] In matters of the faith, this principle means that one helps those being formed to know how to pray, to read the Scriptures and Church documents, and so on – to use those *sources* about which the *Directory* has already written.

If the first pair of attitudes being sought is that of *docibilias and self-formation*, the second attitude the formator is trying to assist in is what the *Directory* calls a "learning by doing". We know that while much learning takes place in formal educational settings it need not be confined to this. St Augustine cites the example of learning languages, pointing out that we learn our mother tongue informally and usually only a second language through the more formal work of a teacher.[222] We learn in a variety of ways: from books, from friends and through our mistakes. Learning is not confined to certain limited, and time-bound, presentations of curricula in school or university. Learning, is simply intrinsic to life. I learn to smile, to shake hands, to open and close a door quietly, to recognise the signs of food in the fridge beginning to mould. I learn to pray, to recognise the signs of a growing friendship, to speak more sensitively, and so

---

[218] G.K. Chesterton, "The Contented Man", in *A Miscellany of Men* (London, Methuen and Co., 1912).

[219] *DC* 135e.

[220] *DC* 135e.

[221] "He who reads to others pronounces the words he recognises; he who teaches reading does so that others may also read." *De Doctrina Christiana* Prol. 9.

[222] St Augustine, *De Doctrina Christiana*. I, I, 5. St Thomas Aquinas, also, distinguishes two ways in which learning takes place: by discovery (*inventio*) and by formal learning (*disciplina*). In the case of *inventio*, one is discovering about the world by oneself. *Questiones disputate de veritate*. James V. McGlynn, S.J. (trans.) (Chicago, Henry Regnery Company, 1953) 11.

on. This is what the *Directory* describes as the "laboratory" of life. Again, though, one needs to be helped to see how to *learn the faith* in this way: through reflecting upon how the Lord is forming one in the midst of life. This question is in large part dealt with in the second part of the *Directory*, in chapter five, looking at God's pedagogy, his education of his people.

Because catechesis is concerned with the communication of the faith *one can also learn constantly from the actual practice of how this is being undertaken*, reflecting on the interactions between the catechist and the learners. Standing before the Lord one can ask key questions about one's catechetical work, undertaking something like a self-examination of conscience after a session:

- How well and thoroughly did I prepare?

- Did I seek to lead others to Christ, to make him the centre of my work, my presentation and any activities or discussion?

- Did I relate in love to those I was with? Did I show Christ-like attentiveness, care and concern for their true good?

- Did I seek to speak the truth in love or only to be well-received and popular?

- Did I do all I could to assist others to learn well, paying attention to how learning takes place?

In this kind of ongoing reflecting one is practising a continual learning by doing of the sort the *Directory* is indicating.

## DIMENSIONS OF FORMATION

We now move from the criteria by which one judges the adequacy of the style of formation to the dimensions, or scope, of that formation. Three dimensions are given which map, naturally enough, onto the character and identify of the catechist that was treated in chapter two: the formation given is to enable the full flourishing of that identity. This part of the chapter, then, has to be read alongside that listing of the characteristics of the catechist:

| IDENTITY OF THE CATECHIST | DIMENSIONS OF FORMATION |
|---|---|
| A witness of faith and keeper of the memory of God | Being and knowing-how-to-be-with |
| A teacher and a mystagogue | Knowledge |
| An accompanier and educator | *Savoir-faire* |

## BEING AND KNOWING-HOW-TO-BE-WITH

The point here is that at the heart of all formation is an understanding that one does not belong to oneself: one *belongs to the Lord*; and he in turn gives us to *belong to others*. When Jesus was asked by the Pharisees whether to pay taxes to Caesar, he responded by reminding them of their primary belonging. God's image was on them (just as Caesar's was on the coin) and so they belonged to God and must give themselves to him (just as the coin belonged to Caesar). Our being made in the image of God means that we are *his*.[223] The catechist in his or her *being* belongs to God. This is the "deepest" level of formation, the one from which all the others flow.[224]

Once one recognises who one is before God, made *for* him, made to belong *intimately* to him, one is able to recognise the sacred identity of those to whom one is in ministry. St John Paul gave beautiful expression to the Church's understanding of the value of every person when he wrote, "the value of one person transcends all the material world".[225] Jesus put it even more starkly: "what does it profit a man, to gain the whole world and forfeit his life?"[226] The life of a person is worth more than the whole world he might seek to possess. The catechist is called to recognise always this incredible value in the person he or she serves, one who is made for nothing less than eternal beatitude.[227]

And there is something more needed: a delicate balance between taking responsibility for those to whom one is in ministry, alongside a deep respect for their "sacred freedom". The early twentieth century poet, Rainer Maria Rilke, wrote several letters to a young man, Franz Xaver Kapus, that capture beautifully what the *Directory* is asking for here, explaining what a relationship "is meant to be between one human being and another...the love that consists in this: the two solitudes protect and border and greet each other".[228] One seeks relationships free from all manipulation and abuse.

We can return to the paradigm of Gabriel and Our Lady to see this played out: on the one hand Gabriel knows his responsibility to communicate the message to the Blessed Virgin, and to do so with all the persuasiveness of a clear proclamation of truth, while witnessing to God's work in her and in others; and at the conclusion of the Annunciation narrative St Luke gives us the simple, yet profound statement, "and the angel departed from her".[229] The role of the angelic catechist was to faithfully *be-with* the Blessed Virgin in a way at once loving, sensitive and intelligent, and then to leave her, in turn, to *be-with* the Lord.

---

223 Cf. *Mark* 12:13-17.
224 *DC* 136, 139.
225 *Christifideles Laici* 37.
226 *Mark* 8:36.
227 Cf. *CCC* 1703.
228 Letter of 14th May 1904, *Letters to a Young Poet,* S. Mitchell (trans.) (Portland, OR, Scriptor Press, 2001) p.26.
229 *Luke* 1:38.

## Knowledge

The *Directory* has looked at the "deepest" element in formation, that of the belonging of the catechist to God and the self-gift of the catechist to others. Now it turns to the question of what the catechist should know and understand. This dimension of knowledge relates to:

- *All that God has revealed*, and which must be transmitted by the catechist
- The *manner in which* the message must be transmitted
- *Those to whom* one hands on the message of hope and salvation

Importantly, to gain this knowledge, the *Directory* refers us to the *sources* that the catechist must know – the Scriptures, the *Catechism of the Catholic Church*, local catechisms and magisterial documents.[230] We can recall that it is by helping those being catechised to directly engage with these "living sources of the faith"[231] that catechesis is renewed. Therefore, a deep familiarity with these sources is the key element in the knowledge that the catechist must be given.

The *Directory* goes on to explain how this knowledge is to be structured for the catechist: in the three main divisions of salvation history – the Old Testament, the New Testament and Church history, with the paschal mystery of Christ as the centre of this history – and in the four areas, or divisions, of the Christian faith – prayer, the sacraments and liturgy, the Creed and life in Christ.[232]

---

[230] *DC* 143.
[231] St John Paul II, *Fidei Depositum* (1992).
[232] The 1997 *GDC* listed these as the "seven foundation stones" of the faith (130).

In addition to developing a curriculum around this basic knowledge, the *Directory* also wants catechists to know "the principal elements of the ecclesial Magisterium concerning the proclamation of Gospel and catechesis".[233] Catechists must be fully aware of the teaching and guidance in this *Directory*, for example, and of key works such as John Paul's *Catechesi Tradendae* and *Fides et Ratio*, Francis's *Evangelii Gaudium*, and Paul VI's *Evangelii Nuntiandi*. The knowledge of these documents is then picked up in the following paragraph, number 145. Here the *Directory* highlights four elements that are treated in magisterial documents and should be included in catechetical formation:

- the *kerygma*
- the narrative outline of the Scriptures
- the ability to provide effective explanations of the faith ("theological content")
- an outline apologetics.

The first item in this list we have already looked into and seen its vital importance. The second, the narrative outline of the Scriptures, we will consider in the next chapter, where it again features strongly. The third element, the ability to provide effective explanations of the faith, is worth a comment here. This and the following point, on apologetics, complement one another. The theological explanations that catechists need to be able to provide refers to their ability to show the relationship of teachings they give to the great themes in *Revelation*, to the *sources* from which they draw, and also to make clear the *interconnectedness* of the doctrines of the faith, to show how the different teachings of the faith make sense together and reinforce one another. So, for instance, the Church's teaching on Mary as the Mother of God does not stand alone, but is intrinsically related to the doctrine that Christ is one divine Person who has taken human nature to himself. Mary is the mother of that divine Person, and so the "Mother of God".

These kinds of explanations, from "within" the faith, drawing upon what God has revealed about himself, are distinct from apologetics, the fourth item. Apologetics is a discipline distinct from catechetics, but closely related to it.[234] It looks at the barriers that can *stand in the way of faith* and that therefore need to be cleared away – especially cultural and intellectual trends inimical to the faith. The *Directory* suggests that some of these barriers may be especially connected to questions of anthropology, widespread misunderstandings of the human person. For example, a false understanding of human freedom runs directly counter to the Christian faith. Many believe that what is supremely valuable in human life is the sheer fact of freedom of choice and that the ability to exercise this, irrespective of the content of

---

[233] *DC* 144.
[234] Cf. *CCC* 6.

choice, is what is especially to be defended. Any objective content – such as God and his wisdom, moral absolutes, or human nature – is seen as potentially threatening to this freedom. It is the unfettered will, the simple act of choice itself, which is to be protected. The Christian view of freedom is very different: we are free not when we choose "anything", but when we are able to choose to fulfil our natures, to find happiness according to who we are as human beings. It is easy to see that unless this distinction is brought out into the open and clarified, areas of formation in the faith will fall onto deaf ears or will meet resistance because of this underlying view that is held that contradicts the faith.

To appreciate what is needed by way of a necessary apologetics we can turn to John Paul II's masterly work, *Fides et Ratio*, "Faith and Reason",[235] in which he wrote of three indispensable foundations that *have* to be in place for the Word of God to be able to be received.[236] The first is what he calls a "sapiential dimension" in one's worldview – that is, the realisation that there is an overarching purpose and meaning in life. We need to know that there is a Mind behind the universe, and that the universe reflects eternal wisdom. Secondly, we need to believe that the human mind can arrive at knowledge of "the very being" of the objects it knows; that we can know things, and that we can know, in some measure, the Truth of the universe itself. And thirdly he argues that the Word of God requires a philosophy of "genuinely metaphysical range". Here, he means essentially that the universe is *worth* knowing, that it is good, that our own most deeply-held values and convictions are not alien to the universe.[237] Many whom we seek to catechise do not have these three convictions firmly in place and catechists can find their work seriously undermined if these are not adequately addressed.

This work on apologetics is related to one further area of knowledge with which the *Directory* concerns itself: all that can be helpful as to how people learn and grow and mature that can be gleaned from the human sciences. These sciences – as all academic disciplines – can carry their own presuppositions about the nature of the human person and the world, which can be compatible, or not, with a Christian worldview, and so the findings cannot be received and used uncritically, as though there were "pure facts" independent of presuppositions. The contributions of these disciplines, therefore, have to be used "*in the perspective of faith and on the basis of Christian anthropology*".[238] Nonetheless, the *Directory* wants to affirm the "valuable contribution" such sciences can make.

---

[235] A work quoted five times in the new *Directory*.

[236] Cf. *FR* 80-83.

[237] *FR* 83. For a discussion of these prerequisites and of their importance for catechesis, cf. C.E. Farey, "Can we Agree on Catechetics?", *Priests and People* 18, 10, Oct. 2004, pp.380-385.

[238] *DC* 147.

The third dimension of formation is that of knowing *how* to communicate, to educate. This section begins with the reminder that whenever we educate in the faith we are working in the realm of God's grace which is "dynamically at work". This is what the Church's calls the "original pedagogy of faith".[239] The phrase goes back to St John Paul II's *Catechesi Tradendae*:

> There is also a pedagogy of faith, and the good that it can do for catechesis cannot be overstated. In fact, it is natural that techniques perfected and tested for education in general should be adapted for the service of education in the faith. However, account must always be taken of the absolute originality of faith. Pedagogy of faith is not a question of transmitting human knowledge, even of the highest kind; it is a question of communicating God's revelation in its entirety. Throughout sacred history, especially in the Gospel, God himself used a pedagogy that must continue to be a model for the pedagogy of faith. A technique is of value in catechesis only to the extent that it serves the faith that is to be transmitted and learned; otherwise it is of no value.[240]

The *Directory* wants to remind the catechist that he or she is "not in charge" of what takes place in catechesis. *God* is in charge, working to elicit and draw out the free response of the participants. Catechesis is the work of the Blessed Trinity in which the catechist is privileged to participate.

That participation is described in the next two paragraphs and a careful reading of the text reveals that the main concern here is to develop in the catechist the capacity for *building mature relationships*, both with individuals and with groups. The catechist is to "look after the quality of the relationships", to "know how to work in communion", to practise "the serene handling of educational relationships", to present salvation history "so that persons may feel part of it", to "guide group dynamics", and so on.[241] The relational aspect of the role of the catechist is again to the fore in the *Directory*, reminding us that catechetics is a discipline concerned with *communication between persons* – *divine* Persons at the heart and centre, yes, and so a mystery and a work of grace, but a work nonetheless in which all human skills of communication are required.

## THE CATECHETICAL FORMATION OF THOSE IN HOLY ORDERS

This short section, paragraphs 151-153, is an addition to the 1997 *Directory*. Both that *Directory* and the current work give consideration to the vital place of those

---

[239] *DC* 148.
[240] *CT* 58.
[241] *DC* 149-150.

in Holy Orders in the section on the role of catechists in different states of life.[242] This current *Directory* now returns to the question of those in Holy Orders in order to reinforce the importance of their pastoral leadership in this area of Church life. The aim of this reinforcement is clearly stated: "to foster a greater and more direct involvement of priests into catechetical action" and to enable them to be involved "in the formative activity of catechists."[243] The catechetical formation they need should be provided in the formal programmes preparing them for Holy Orders, but should not end there: it should appear "above all in the context of their ongoing formation".[244] That view is consistent with the strong presentation in the *Directory* of our lives as a "laboratory" in which God continues to teach us, and it also coheres with the equally clear emphasis placed on the unity of witness, teaching and pastoral life – a formation in which these can be brought together will arguably be able to provide a more effective form of learning than one in which studies are detached from their immediate ministerial context.

Regarding the curriculum for these studies, the *Directory* first states that the same criteria for formation presented in the *Directory* – providing what we can call the "style" of the formation – apply here.[245] It then goes on to identify particular elements of catechetical understanding that are especially important for those in Holy Orders

---

[242] *GDC* 222-225; *DC* 114-118.
[243] *DC* 153.
[244] *DC* 153.
[245] The passage is referring us back to *DC* 135.

because of the teaching and homiletic roles that priests and deacons have.[246] Two items that are crucial are a thorough knowledge of the *Catechism* and of the *Rite of Christian Initiation of Adults*, the first of these – as we shall see – expressing the teaching of the Church according to the pedagogy of God, and thus providing the basic model for catechetical presentations; the second expressing the catechumenal model which is paradigmatic for catechesis.[247] Alongside a formal study of catechetics according to the Magisterium those in formation are also be to given "experiences of the first proclamation" – the *kerygma* should be regularly presented – and "exercises in the various forms of catechesis" – in other words, practical, hands-on forms of learning of this craft.

## CENTRES OF FORMATION

The final section of this chapter deals with centres where catechetical formation is offered. Three types are distinguished, differentiated by level. The text stresses the importance in each case of ensuring that the centres provide *high quality* formation, as befits this vital ministry of the Church. This quality depends upon "the use of specialist formators" who also have "good pastoral experience and sensibility". Those well-formed in the discipline of catechetics who also have considerable field experience are needed to lead this kind of formation.[248]

The levels of the centres can be seen as cumulative, each building on the other. In the first kind of centre, for the "basic formation of catechists", what is emphasised is the need for a formation that is systematic and comprehensive. These centres can be established at the parish, the "interparochial", or the diocesan level. As we saw earlier, the *Directory* wants formation to be undertaken in as *local* a manner as possible, so that the formation given can be provided in the context of the reality of sustained relationships and accompaniment.

In the second kind of centre, intended for "officials and leaders of catechesis", the emphasis falls on forming those who can in turn form others, whether at parish, interparochial or deanery level – or even diocesan. A focus is provided on developing a breadth of study in terms of academic disciplines, the period of study is more extensive, and the curriculum orientated towards providing the competence needed to form other catechists. The *Directory* reiterates the need for this formation to be provided according to the general criteria we have already noted, especially by providing the

---

[246] The points given in paragraph 152 make more explicit or amplify items identified in the "Ratio fundamentalis institutionis sacerdotalis" (2016), the basic plan of priestly formation issued by the Congregation for the Clergy.

[247] On the place of the *Catechism* in seminary studies, cf. E. Westby, "The *Catechism of the Catholic Church* and the Theologate", in P. Willey and S. Sollom (eds), *Speaking the Truth in Love: The Catechism and the New Evangelisation*, Steubenville: Emmaus Academic 2019, pp.475-492.

[248] Cf. *DC* 154.

experience of ongoing accompaniment in the studies. Receiving formation of this kind reinforces the need to provide this same experience for those who they in turn will support in their development towards catechetical maturity. These centres, of necessity, are established at the diocesan, interdiocesan or national level.

In the third kind of formation centre the emphasis shifts again. In this kind, "for experts in catechetics", we find the *Directory* using the term for the study of an academic discipline, "catechetics", rather than the practice of transmitting the faith. As we have noted, *the levels are cumulative*: one begins with a systematic, well-rounded and comprehensive formation for being a catechist; then the next level, building on this, adds to it the capacity to form others to undertake catechetical work, drawing in additional disciplines as needed for this competency. Finally, one studies the perennial principles of catechetics. This kind of centre forms those who will be able – in addition to forming catechists – to provide the co-ordination of catechesis at a diocesan level, undertake research in catechetics and lead centres of catechetical formation.

## QUESTIONS FOR REFLECTION

1 In what areas is the Holy Spirit prompting me to seek more formation:
  in being-with God and others?
  • in knowledge?
  • in knowing the craft of catechesis, of how to hand on the faith to others?
2 Where do I sense in myself areas of uncertainty, of nervousness?
  • Am I open to be formed?
  • How might I practically take steps to find this formation?

# A Prayer for Catechists

HOLY SPIRIT,
Guide and counsellor,
Intimate friend and purifier of our lives,
Be with us to lead us to courageously seek
The formation we need for our ministry,
To give ourselves generously to this task.
We ask this in the name of him who gave his all for us,
Jesus Christ, our Lord.
Amen.

# CHAPTER V

# The Pedagogy of the Faith

This central part of the *Directory* is called "The Process of Catechesis" and consists of four chapters. It opens with the great truths about how God educates us (chapter five) and then unpacks how the *Catechism of the Catholic Church* is a faithful expression of that educational activity (chapter six). The *Directory* then moves on to consider the different elements and methods that can be used in catechesis and how to evaluate each of them in the light of God's pedagogy (chapter seven). Finally, detailed consideration is given to each of the different groups of people who need to receive the saving truths of the faith, the Good News of Christ Jesus (chapter eight).

Succinctly and carefully, this opening chapter, "The Pedagogy of the Faith", sets before us the *perennial principles* that govern catechesis whenever and wherever that catechesis takes place. These universally-valid principles for the transmission of the faith form what is described as an "original pedagogy" for the Church's work of catechesis. They are derived from a contemplation on how *God acts towards us* to communicate his life to us.

But the chapter does even more than provide us with these principles. As it does so it *lifts our vision of catechesis,* inviting us to gaze on the activity of God himself, helping us to understand that *he himself* is the catechist of every person and of the human race. Our vision is first focused in this chapter, then, on the reality underpinning these essential principles, that is, on the engagement of God himself in the work of catechesis that is fundamentally his. When we hand on the faith to others we are not seeking to make our work accord simply with stimulating ideas or inspiring ideals for living. In catechesis we are taking our reference point from the truth of who God *Is* and how he comes to us, reaching down into our lives (the tradition of the Church calls this his "condescension") in order to lift us up to share in his unbounded and everlasting love.

The phrase used for God's catechetical work in our lives is the "divine pedagogy". We are used to the word "pedagogy" signifying something like an educational methodology, and so "divine pedagogy" might sound to us as though it is something of only limited importance. But in fact the *Directory* ties it to the most all-embracing fact of all – that of God's Revelation of himself for our salvation. The opening of the chapter asks us to revise our understanding of the term in this way:

> Revelation is the great educational work of God. In fact, it can also be interpreted through a pedagogical lens. In it we find the distinctive elements that can help lead us to recognise a *divine pedagogy*, one which is capable of profoundly influencing the Church's educational activity. Catechesis also follows in the footsteps of God's pedagogy.[249]

Revelation is God's great *educational* work, his great work of *pedagogy*. He reveals himself to us in order to instruct us about himself so that we would come to understand who he is in order to enter into his life.

The word "pedagogy" is worth dwelling on further. It signifies not so much a teaching role in education as *an accompanying and formative role*. The word is taken from the Greek *pedagogos*, and refers to one who has care of a child. Literally, it means one who "leads the child". In ancient Greek and Roman culture the pedagogue would be the figure – usually a slave – who would be tasked with accompanying the young child of the family to and from school. The pedagogue would see to it that each child remained attentive at school and, once home, would supervise the child's behaviour and habits, disciplining the child as needed. The focus of the work of the pedagogue was the formation of character through establishing a personal relationship with the growing child, as well as an integration of the studies learned at school with the virtues and qualities of character expected in the family household. It was the role of the pedagogue, then, to *help the child to learn* and *to put into practice* that which was given by the teacher.

When we speak of the "divine pedagogy", then, we are referring especially to the activity of God in the role of pedagogue. God is the supreme Teacher of humanity who imparts his wisdom and at the same time, he is also the pedagogue of the human race, the one who "leads the child".[250] God sets about forming our characters, helping us

---

[249] *DC* 157.
[250] For the background in ancient Romano-Greco culture, cf. H.I. Marrou, *A History of Education in Antiquity* (London, Sheed and Ward 1956) 142-149, and W. Jaeger *Early Christianity and Greek Paideia* (Cambridge, Harvard University Press 1965).

to learn what is necessary for growing up well in *his* household. It is surely significant that Paul speaks of Christ taking the form of the slave and that Jesus highlights his relationship to his disciples as that of being the servant as he prepares his disciples to dwell in the home of the Father.[251] The *Directory* describes the pedagogy of the faith as being "inspired by the self-abasement of God".[252]

By placing this chapter at the centre of the *Directory*, then, the Church is asking us to be attentive to God's *own* formative work in each person. The opening paragraphs of this chapter ask us to read the history of God's relationship with the human race in and through this focus on formation, understanding ourselves as his children in need of being brought to maturity through a divine work of formation and discipline.[253]

A rich Trinitarian presentation of this pedagogy is presented here as the *Directory* walks us through the pedagogy of the Father,[254] the Son,[255] and the Holy Spirit.[256] At the heart of this presentation we are introduced to the pedagogy of *Jesus* as one who follows a style of accompaniment and gradual formation of his disciples. The *Directory* also shows us how Jesus undertakes each of the five tasks of catechesis with his disciples: thus, he *explains his teachings* to them in "depth", "leads them to the experience of the *Eucharist*", "taught them the truth through his whole *life*", "introduced them to *prayer*", and walked with them so as to send them out "as a little *community*".[257] The basis for the five tasks of catechesis can be found in Jesus's own pedagogy. The *Holy Spirit*, meanwhile, is beautifully depicted as the *indwelling Pedagogue* of each person, "conforming them to the Son by bringing them every gift of grace" and enabling them to call God *Father*.[258] This pedagogy of the Persons of the Trinity, the *Directory* notes, comes together in a particular way at the point of the Annunciation, where we see the pedagogical work of the Persons fulfilled in Mary's "full response of faith".[259] The *Directory* says that we can in fact sum up catechetical pedagogy as the "pedagogy of the Incarnation".[260]

This opening section of the chapter, then, has reminded us of the primacy of *God's agency* in the work of catechesis and formation, an interwoven Trinitarian work of great

---

[251] Cf. *Philippians* 2:7; *John* 13:2ff.; 14:2.

[252] *DC* 179.

[253] The *Directory* sends us to biblical passages such as *Deuteronomy* 8:5; *Hosea* 11:3-4 and *Proverbs* 3:11-12, passages characterised by *loving discipline*.

[254] *DC* 158.

[255] *DC* 159-161.

[256] *DC* 162-163.

[257] *DC* 160. Emphasis added.

[258] *DC* 162-163. The *Catechism* picks up this depiction of the Holy Spirit in *CCC* 1697: "the interior Master of life according to Christ, a gentle guest and friend who inspires, guides, corrects, and strengthens this life".

[259] *DC* 159.

[260] *DC* 165. For the continuity of this point with previous teaching cf. also *GDC* 143.

grace and love for our lives that calls us to maturity in the faith, providing a model of unlooked-for condescension and personal care to inspire our work of catechesis.

## PEDAGOGY IN THE FAITH OF THE CHURCH

How is this truth of God's primacy in evangelisation and catechesis reflected in the Church and in the ministry of catechesis?

The Second Vatican Council's document on Divine Revelation, *Dei Verbum* says that "In the sacred books, the Father who is in heaven comes lovingly to meet his children and talks with them".[261] How do we *learn to hear and to understand* these words of our heavenly Father? For this understanding, the *Directory* directs us to our *Mother, the Church.*[262] And the *Catechism* tells us: "As a mother who teaches her children to speak and so to understand and communicate, the Church our Mother teaches us the language of faith in order to introduce us to the understanding and the life of faith."[263] It is through the pedagogy of the Church our Mother, then, that we are led to hear and to understand the Father's Word.

The *Directory* describes the Church as a "visible and actual continuation of the pedagogy of the Father and the Son".[264] This continuation is not to be thought of as a replacement, as though the Church now stands in the place of God and has taken over his role as Pedagogue of his people. The *Directory* uses the term "locus". The Church, as his Bride, is the place where the pedagogy of God is received, the sphere in which his formative and saving activity takes place, the clear spring from which his cleansing waters flow. And the healing flow of this learning and formation down through the centuries is expressed beautifully in the *Directory*:

> Throughout the centuries the Church has produced an incomparable treasure of pedagogy in the faith: above all the witness of saints and catechists; a variety of ways of life and original forms of religious communication such as the catechumenate, catechisms, itineraries of Christian life; a precious patrimony of catechetical teaching of faith culture, of catechetical institutions and services.[265]

The history of the Church reveals how the "dialogue of salvation" between God and humanity takes place. The Church continues the pedagogy of God by being the place in which the sources of grace, freely given, are *received*,[266] where his wisdom is *learned*,

---

[261] Second Vatican Council, *Dei Verbum* (1965): 21.
[262] *DC* 164. Scripture, too, speaks of the Father and the mother assisting us together in this regard: "Hear, my son, your father's instruction, and reject not your mother's teaching; for they are a fair garland for your head, and pendants for your neck" (*Proverbs* 1:8-9).
[263] *CCC* 171.
[264] *DC* 164.
[265] *DC* 164.
[266] Cf. *DC* 90-109.

where his gifts are welcomed and *practised* and his abundant love and saving truth is *handed on.*

Drawing on the sources for catechesis and on the history of the Church, the *Directory* now identifies the *perennial principles* that the Church follows in her catechetical work in order to ensure that it keeps the character of the "original pedagogy of faith". The *Directory* calls these the "criteria for the proclamation of the evangelical message". These are not new or unexpected principles but are essentially an unpacking and making explicit of what has been presented in the earlier section on the pedagogy of God. Five central principles are offered to us here:

- The Trinitarian and Christological criterion
- The criterion of salvation history
- The criterion of the primacy of grace and of beauty
- The criterion of ecclesiality
- The criterion of the unity and integrity of the faith

We can look at each in turn.

## THE TRINITARIAN AND CHRISTOLOGICAL CRITERION

This is rightly expressed as a single criterion rather than two separate criteria. The *Directory* puts it this way: catechesis is Christocentric because "Christ is the way that leads to the intimate mystery of God".[267] Jesus is the full Revelation of the Father and the Way to come to know him. The Father asks us to listen to Christ because Jesus's whole being is open to receive whatever the Father wishes to give him. Therefore, in the Gospels we see one of his main titles is simply "Son" – not a proper name, but a term describing his position in a *relationship*, showing that his identity is entirely rooted in the Father. Christ does not preach himself, but only the Father. It is the Holy Spirit bestowed by Christ on his disciples, in turn, who enables us to know that Jesus is the Lord and to gaze upon his face.[268] When the *Directory*, then, unpacks a range of ways in which catechesis is Christocentric, in order to maintain the character of the "original pedagogy of faith", it intends us to understand this as a *Trinitarian-Christocentricity* in each case – that is, it is speaking always of Christ-in-relation-to-his-Father-and his Spirit.

The concept of Christocentricity is a rich one, and the *Directory* identifies four ways in which the centrality of Christ needs to be recognised and maintained in catechesis.

- He is the "living, present and active" centre of catechesis. When a catechist and learner are together they are in the presence of the Risen Lord, and both need an attitude of docility to his activity in their midst.

---

[267] *DC* 168.
[268] Cf. *John* 14:6, 9-10; 20:22; *2 Corinthians* 3:17-18.

- He is the key for understanding every teaching, both in the sense that all of the figures, feasts and institutions from salvation history point to him, and because revealing his presence and centrality to each teaching unveils the personal core of every doctrine, preventing it from being thought of as a "thing" or abstract truth, rather than a living aspect of his own Being.

- He is the focal point of all history (as the Liturgy of Eater Vigil has it, "all time belongs to him and all the ages") and of every individual person's life. We divide all time by reference to him, marking it either "Before Christ", B.C. or "Anno Domini", A.D., the Year of the Lord. The *Directory* explains how a catechesis based on the mysteries of Christ – the events of his life celebrated in the liturgy – enables each individual person to enter into his life, into those events understood "in their perennial theological and spiritual sense".[269] Thus each of us is enabled to join ourselves to the centre and key point of all human history and realise that our own lives, too, are held secure in that Centre.

- His teaching and pedagogy, as the teaching and pedagogy of God himself, is the constant reference point for our catechesis. All that we hand on is enlightened by his actions and words, and especially of course, his paschal mystery.

---

[269] *DC* 170.

## THE CRITERION OF SALVATION HISTORY

Christ is the living centre of salvation history and at the heart of catechesis is the telling of "the story" of God's deeds in history.[270] The term for this in the catechetical tradition of the Church is the *narratio*, the narrative of the faith. What do we mean by this? If you read through the Book of Psalms what is apparent is that many of them recount the story of what happened to the Israelites at the Exodus from Egypt. They remember the time of slavery in Egypt, the miracles by which God persuaded Pharaoh to let them leave to worship him in the desert, the saving of the people at the Red Sea and the journey to the meeting with God at Mount Sinai where he made a covenant with them; then the journey to the Promised Land, their lack of faith in him which led to the wilderness wanderings, and finally their settling in the new land of Canaan. This story, with all of its drama, is told over and again. The psalms were written several hundred years later and yet this remains the *story* of Israel. When eventually they are taken into slavery again, taken into exile in Babylon, returning several generations later, this later event is also cast in Exodus terms. It is a second exodus from slavery. This, then, is the essential Jewish *narratio*, the community story that is passed down through the generations, the story that everyone knows, the story that shapes the collective psyche of the nation. The story is told in the psalms; it is also recalled in her liturgical feasts, especially in the Feasts of the Passover, of Tabernacles and the Feast of Weeks. And, of course, the story is told in the family, as parents pass this account on to their children.

Other peoples and cultures have comparable stories of this fundamental kind, those accounts that have shaped the nation, that everyone knows, that help define what it is to be a member of that people. For example, England has essentially an "island story" and, while there are variants on this, her story is fundamentally one of defending an island against potential invaders in different forms. Sometimes the invaders are successful and then they become part of the story of the next defence. But the collective psyche of English people is shaped by this overall type of story, with major points being especially important (the invasion of the Romans, the Danes and the Normans, and then in past centuries the unsuccessful attempts of the Spanish, French and the Germans). One of the reasons the Reformation took such a strong hold in England is probably that the Reformers harnessed this story that was so deeply embedded in the English psyche and turned it against Catholics so that Catholics became foreigners on their own soil, mere representatives of a foreign and threatening power.

What about Christians? What is the essential *narratio* that *Christians* must know and hand on, to form and shape each generation? This story is what catechists must echo as they become the "story tellers" of the People of God. As we know, it is a story centred on the Incarnation and paschal mystery, on Christmas and Easter. Dorothy

---

[270] *DC* 171-173, and cf. also 74, 144-145, 149.

Sayers rightly called it "the most exciting drama that ever staggered the imagination".[271] G.K. Chesterton called it "that incredible interruption...the blow that broke the very backbone of history".[272] The Good News comes to us as a *narrative*. It is the story of the Second Person of the Blessed Trinity assuming our human nature, living among us to heal and teach us and then dying on the Cross and rising from the dead to release us from the power of Satan, death and sin. It is a story unique in the history of the world because it is the story of *God himself* appearing in time and in the flesh and blood of our nature. It is the only story told about God that is *literally* historical.

This story fulfils, as it must, the story told in what the Church calls "the time of the promises" – that is, the time of the Jewish people before the advent of Jesus; it gathers up and transfigures this story, showing us clearly all that it meant: the time in Egypt is now fulfilled in Jesus's coming out of Egypt as a child, which in turn prefigures his "passover" in Jerusalem as the lamb of sacrifice, passing over from death into life. On this passover journey he spends time tempted in the desert, he acts as the new Moses, and he bestows the new Law. Everything in that original story is now seen as what the Church calls a "type" of Christ – it is an image that finds its *reality* and *full meaning* in him.[273]

Knowing this *narratio* of Christ's life, death and resurrection is foundational for the catechist. Frank Sheed puts it this way,

> The teacher of Religion should be absolutely soaked in the New Testament, so that she knows what every key chapter is about; knows the line of thought of every book of it, could find her way about it blindfold. That seems to me an indispensable minimum.[274]

The centre of the *narratio* is Christ. He recapitulates in himself the whole story of Israel and fulfils it. And he does even more. He fulfils the story of *every* people and every individual person, for Jesus is the new *Adam*. Pilate introduces him to the crowd that seek his death by saying, "Behold the Man".[275] Jesus is the new Adam, the last Adam, the Adam who is from heaven and who takes all that was in the first Adam and brings it to spiritual fulfilment, to the "ultimate horizon" of eternal life.[276] The Second Vatican Council taught,

> He who is 'the image of the invisible God' (*Colossians* 1:15), is himself the perfect man. To the sons of Adam he restores the divine likeness which had been disfigured

---

[271] Dorothy Sayers, *Creed or Chaos* (London, Methuen and Co. Ltd., 1947) p.1.

[272] G.K. Chesterton, *The Everlasting Man,* in *G.K. Chesterton: Collected Works Volume II* (San Francisco, Ignatius Press, 1986) p.401.

[273] Cf. *DC* 170.

[274] Frank Sheed, *Are we Really Teaching Religion?* (London, Sheed and Ward, 1953) III, i.

[275] *John* 19:5. In Greek, it is "behold Adam".

[276] *DC* 173, cf. *1 Corinthians* 15:45-49.

from the first sin onward. Since human nature as he assumed it was not annulled, by that very fact it has been raised up to a divine dignity in our respect too. For by his incarnation the Son of God has united himself in some fashion with every man.[277]

We never move "beyond" Christ. All we can do is to enter more and more deeply into the reality and truth of who he is. The *Catechism* quotes from St John of the Cross in this connection:

In giving us his Son, his only Word (for he possesses no other), he spoke everything to us at once in this sole Word – and he has no more to say...because what he spoke before to the prophets in parts, he has now spoken all at once by giving us the All Who is his Son. Any person questioning God or desiring some vision or revelation would be guilty not only of foolish behaviour but also of offending him, by not fixing his eyes entirely upon Christ and by living with the desire for some other novelty.[278]

---

[277] Second Vatican Council, *Gaudium et Spes* (1965): 22.

[278] St John of the Cross, "The Ascent of Mount Carmel" 2, 22, 3-5 in *The Collected Works of St John of the Cross*, K. Kavanaugh OCD and O. Rodriguez OCD (trans.), (Washington DC, Institute of Carmelite Studies, 1979) 179-180; quoted in *CCC* 65. For this reason, when the *Directory* speaks of the "progressive nature of Revelation" (*DC* 165) it is not referring to any Revelation beyond or after Christ, but the way in which God's progressive Revelation through the ages was brought to fulfilment in Christ in history.

This narratio, then, is a "principle of hope for the whole world and for the people of every time".[279] Precisely because Jesus is the new Adam, the story of Jesus is the story to which *every* person can rightly unite him or herself and find their true identity there. Catechists, therefore, tell the *narratio* as *our* story, as the story that shapes the Church's self-understanding and identity, in which every person can find his or her place.

The *narratio* is handed on by catechists. Parents, as the first catechists of their children, have the responsibility of handing on this story in the home, while those in ordained ministry have the chief role in passing this on by teaching and proclamation – and also through the liturgy, for the Eucharist, of course, is the fulfilment of the Feast of the Passover and is the place *par excellence* for the handing of the story. In the Mass, the *narratio* appears as fulfilled in the readings from the Scriptures, and the story is also told in summary fashion in the Creed. Each person sharing in the divine Sacrifice of the Mass is united to Jesus and to all the living and dead (though none are dead who are in him) in and through their union with Jesus's passing over to the Father. There we are made one with him, a union which will be fulfilled finally "at table in God's kingdom".[280]

## THE CRITERION OF THE PRIMACY OF GRACE AND OF BEAUTY

Uniting grace and beauty into a single criterion helps us to appreciate that when the Church speaks of beauty she is not thinking primarily of an aesthetic quality, but is drawing attention to God himself. And so the *Directory* points us to the beauty of the life and actions of Christ, the One who is God among us. *In us, the eternal beauty of God appears as grace, as the life of God in us.* This is manifested in us as the beauty of *holiness*, the beauty of Our Lady and of the saints, The Blessed Virgin is spoken of in the Church's tradition as the *tota pulchra*, the "all-beautiful", and this is precisely because she is full of grace.[281] Beauty appears in us as the creaturely response to God's grace.

Grace is the life of God, and he always gives of himself freely and out of love. This life was bestowed in and through Christ: "from his fullness have we all received, grace upon grace".[282] It is given as a free gift and the work of grace also sustains the human response to that loving initiative: "man must have the grace of God to move and assist him; he must have the interior helps of the Holy Spirit, who moves the heart and converts it to God, who opens the eyes of the mind and 'makes it easy for all to accept and believe the truth.'"[283] In one sense, then, the work is all *his*; it is all the work of that original Beauty, of grace. And yet the wonder of grace

---

[279] *DC* 172.
[280] *DC* 173.
[281] Cf. *Luke* 1:28.
[282] *John* 1:16.
[283] *CCC* 153, quoting from Second Vatican Council, *Dei Verbum* (1965): 5.

is that it does not exclude human collaboration or make it redundant, but rather underpins and enables it. God's beauty reveals itself as one that desires and enables free collaboration with creatures.

The *Directory* emphasises the importance of this criterion for catechesis as one that enables us to keep an appropriate balance in our presentation of the faith, keeping the focus on God's work rather than our own and also helping those whom we catechise understand that the demands and challenges of the Christian life are anticipated by our Father who also gives all the grace we need in order to meet them. Catechists are asked to lead in their presentations not with what *we* need to do, but with all that God does, focusing attention on his grace and initiative, reminding those to whom they minister that "it is by grace that our works can bear fruit for eternal life."[284] In this way, presentations we make on the moral life, in particular, are *made beautiful*, for the moral life is the life of grace in us, the life of holiness, of being united to God's loving grace.[285]

## THE CRITERION OF ECCLESIALITY

Quoting from the 1997 *Directory*, the text of this document returns to one of its favourite themes, that of the ecclesial nature of catechesis – the fact that as a catechist one lives and speaks not in isolation, but on behalf of and as a member of the great body of believers stretching through time and space. Our story is found in the story of the People of God and our ministry, likewise, is never set apart from the ministry of that whole Body. The ministry of the catechist flows from this communion with believers and helps others to enter more deeply into it.[286] This principle, then, acts as a reminder that, as catechists, we *receive* our mission to teach and educate from the Church and that we do so under her *authority* and with the *spiritual support* of the saints and martyrs.

This criterion is inseparable from the first, from that of Christocentricity. We can recall the crucial doctrine of the faith, *Christus totus* – the *whole*, or complete, Christ. Catechists are members of Christ's living Body, in communion with him as branches in a vine, receiving in the vine *his* own life which enables them to bear the fruit of love and sound teaching.[287] In and through that communion with Christ in the Holy

---

[284] *DC* 174, quoting *CCC* 1697.

[285] Cf. *DC* 175, which is here picking up earlier points in the *Directory*. For example, it has been emphasised already that catechists should teach that "God's saving love...precedes any moral and religious obligation on our part" (59). Presentations on the moral life, which are so fundamental a part of what catechists need to hand on (cf. *DC* 84, 93, 104, 144, 169, and so on) can shine out with examples of the beauty of the holiness of the saints once they are set in the context of God's saving grace (cf. also *DC* 141).

[286] *DC* 176.

[287] Cf. the image in *John* 15 of the vine and the branches that Jesus uses to speak of the close communion of his disciples with him.

Spirit, catechists are also profoundly united to all of the other members of Christ, other "branches" attached to the one vine, enjoying union with all other members of the one Church. Joseph Ratzinger put it like this: "In the Eucharist I can never demand communion with Jesus alone. He has given himself a Body. Whoever receives him in Communion necessarily communicates with all his brothers and sisters who have become members of the one Body."[288]

## THE CRITERION OF THE UNITY AND INTEGRITY OF THE FAITH

This final criterion is a deeply respectful one. The catechist is not to think of himself as the arbiter of the truth, as a kind of gatekeeper between God and the person, taking upon himself the ultimate authority in catechesis with a responsibility for adapting, altering or reducing the divine deposit in any way. Such an attitude, however well-meaning in intention it might be, is identified by the *Directory* as a form of *gnosis* – a reference here to ancient religious sects prevalent in the early centuries of Christianity who reserved areas of teaching to those judged to be the "elect". It is perhaps a common temptation for those in ministry to judge that lives are too broken or disordered to receive the Church's message. This criterion reminds us that, on the contrary, Christ's message is for *all* and is proclaimed in its *fullness* as *good news for the poor*.[289] There is no one who is to be excluded from receiving the fullness of the Church's teaching. The only limitations to the fullness of the Good News being received will come, the *Directory* indicates, from how far each person "is able to receive it",[290] to welcome God's free gift of his life and grace and make room for Christ's loving truth.

The attitude of respect called for is not only that which is directed towards learners, towards those who have a right to receive the teaching of Christ "not in mutilated, falsified or diminished form but whole and entire",[291] but is also – and most importantly – directed towards God. Catechists speak *his* Word, *his* truth. "All revealed truths derive from the same divine source"[292] and catechists owe their primary allegiance to him to transmit the faith in its integrity.

That integrity, moreover, is necessary because the faith forms a single unity. Every truth of the faith is united to every other one, making up a single whole. Such a unity might be thought of as a single body made up of many parts, with the unity being an organic, living one in which the richness of the whole is accessed and made available through the many parts. Some of the Fathers of the Church used the image of Christ's seamless garment to express this truth. The *Directory* speaks of the unity of the faith in terms of its origin: it is rooted in a "hierarchy" – a sacred structure – with certain of the

---

288 Joseph Ratzinger, *Called to Communion* (San Francisco, Ignatius Press, 1996) p.82.
289 Cf. also *CCC* 543-545.
290 *DC* 177.
291 *DC* 177, citing *CT* 30.
292 *DC* 178, citing *EG* 36.

truths lying, as it were, closer to the divine Source, with other truths being dependent upon them. Thus, they are held together ultimately in the Unity of God himself, with that Unity flowing down through all of the truths.

Holding together unity and integrity is helpful for the catechist since so often there seem to be so many things to teach and one wants to do justice to them all. It is helpful for the catechist to be able to explain that when one touches any part of the seamless garment one is in touch with the whole of the faith – and, most importantly, that one is in touch with Christ himself, the One in whom all things hold together.[293]

## CATECHETICAL PEDAGOGY

The final section of this chapter on pedagogy – on identifying the perennial principles of the transmission of the faith, foremost among which is the reality of God's work as both Teacher and Pedagogue – concerns the distinction and relationship of the divine and the human in the work of catechesis.

We must not confuse God's work and our own, grace and human effort. We have already seen that "Catechesis must avoid identifying the salvific action of God with human pedagogical action".[294] Two realities are involved in catechesis, the divine and the human. Yet catechesis follows a "pedagogy of the Incarnation",[295] as we have

---

[293] Cf. *Colossians* 1:15.
[294] *DC* 181.
[295] *DC* 165.

seen, and in the Incarnation of the Lord the divine and human are united while not being confused. Our pedagogy is centred on Christ who, as the divine Son, assumed the human, and transfigured and glorified that same humanity. In and through Christ all that is human is capable of that same transfigured service of the divine. And so this section speaks of a "twofold fidelity – to God and to humanity"[296] and explains how all of the capacities of human work, thinking and intelligence can play their own important part in the work of catechesis. The human sciences also have an important role – and the *Directory* highlights here the disciplines of education, communication and psychology. Their contribution to catechesis is, in fact, "indispensable".[297] Just as Christ assumed human nature, so in catechesis the faith "assumes" all that is human, evaluating it and "reinterpreting these contributions from the perspective of Revelation."[298] All that is authentically human in this work of catechesis is destined for its fulfilment by being taken up in Christ in and through his Church.

## QUESTIONS FOR REFLECTION

1   Do I allow God to *Father* me?
   - Do I allow Jesus to *form* me?
   - Do I allow the Holy Spirit to *strengthen* me and *give me hope*?
   - Do I allow the Church, my mother, to *teach* and *guide* me?

2   In my ministry which of the essential criteria am I consciously building into my catechesis?
   - Do I try to make Jesus Christ the heart of all I do and say?
   - Do I highlight the truth that God, Father, Son and Holy Spirit, is the centre and light of every teaching I give?

---

[296] *DC* 179.
[297] *DC* 180.
[298] *DC* 180.

# A Prayer for Catechists

MARY,

Mother of catechists and Mother of the Church,

You gave yourself without reserve into the hands of God

And received the divine Son in his fullness into your life.

Intercede for us now,

Asking for the grace we need in our lives

To trustingly abandon ourselves to God's will

So that he can form us and bring

Christ to birth in our lives also.

We ask this in the name of your Son Jesus.

Amen.

# CHAPTER VI:

# The *Catechism of the Catholic Church*

The first thing that is interesting to note about this chapter is *where* it is placed in the ordering of the *Directory*: it directly follows the chapter on the pedagogy of God in which God's ways of educating his people is presented to us and then translated into a series of perennial principles for transmitting the faith in catechesis. This chapter on the *Catechism* is positioned here in the *Directory* because "The content of the *Catechism* is presented in such a way as to manifest the pedagogy of God."[299] The way in which the faith is structured and expounded in the *Catechism*, in other words, is a faithful reflection of God's pedagogy – which, as we know, is the inspiration for all catechesis. The *Catechism* is the work which can be placed in the hands of catechists to assist them in learning this pedagogy so as to be inspired by it in their own ministry.

To help us to focus on the significance of this point, we can compare the current *Directory* with its predecessor. In the 1997 *General Directory for Catechesis* the chapter on the *Catechism* was placed within a part called "The Gospel Message". This was a natural positioning to highlight the contribution of the *Catechism*. For it is true, of course, that the *Catechism* ensures that all involved in catechesis have in this text a solid reference point with regard to *content*, with the announcing and explaining of the truths of the faith. When the 1997 *Directory* was composed, it was vital that this central point about the *Catechism* be firmly established, especially since there

---

[299] *DC* 192.

had been significant confusion and considerable dissent with respect to what the Church teaches on different topics. The publication of the *Catechism* meant that there was a definitive account to which all catechists could turn in order to know what are "the events and fundamental salvific truths which express the faith".[300] Thus the 1997 *Directory* emphasised the point that the *Catechism* "synthesises normatively the totality of the Catholic faith."[301]

In the present *Directory*, an additional feature of the *Catechism* is now being drawn out to be made clearer, which we can see reflected in this choice of where the chapter on the *Catechism* is placed. This point is that *the way in which* the content of the faith is presented in the *Catechism* expresses the perennial principles of catechesis. The *Catechism* does not only provide a definitive guide with regard to content. It does the same with regard to catechetical pedagogy.

A careful reading of St John Paul II's introduction to the *Catechism*, *Fidei Depositum*, in fact reveals the presence of this pedagogical purpose. The *Catechism* is declared by St John Paul II to be a "sure norm for *teaching* the faith".[302] This point corrects a view of the *Catechism* that would see it simply as a kind of reference tool for looking up matters on which one needs clarification, as something like a modern encyclopedia of the faith's contents. Certainly, the *Catechism* offers this for catechists. Nonetheless, this limited way of looking at the *Catechism* overlooks the fact that it has been written and promulgated to serve the *teaching* of the faith to others and that everything in the *Catechism* is to assist with that overarching purpose, including not only the *clarity* with which it presents saving doctrine but also, for example, the *tone* with which doctrines are introduced, their *placing and ordering* in relation to one another, the way in which *sources* are introduced, and so on – all matters that are important for catechists to consider as they approach the work of faithfully handing on the precious deposit of faith.[303] The focus in this chapter, therefore, is placed on what the *Directory* calls the "theological-catechetical significance of the *Catechism*".[304]

## HISTORICAL NOTE

An introductory historical note places the *Catechism* in the mainstream of the Church's life. It first reminds us of the ecclesial tradition of producing summaries of the faith. These summaries were gathered in both question and answer format, as in the

---

[300] *DC* 184, citing *GDC* 124.

[301] *GDC* no.120.

[302] Emphasis added. In Latin, the phrase is *firmam regulam ad fidem docendam*.

[303] The need for this aspect of the *Catechism* to be more deeply received is discussed by C.E. Farey in "Reception of the *Catechism of the Catholic Church*", in Reno Fisichella, *The Catechism of the Catholic Church with Theological Commentary* (Huntingdon, Indiana, Our Sunday Visitor, 2020) pp.581-594.

[304] *DC* 190.

interrogatory questions in the *Rite of Baptism*, and in expository and declarative form, as in the early creeds and the present *Catechism*. We find in these different summaries combinations and elaborations of the earliest proclamations about Christ – "Jesus is Lord", "He was raised on the third day", and so on, which we see, for example in Paul's *First Letter to the Corinthians*:

> For I delivered to you as of first importance what I also received, that Christ died for our sins in accordance with the scriptures, that he was buried, that he was raised on the third day in accordance with the scriptures, and that he appeared to Cephas, then to the twelve.[305]

While universal catechisms would not be written until the sixteenth century, the gathering of "summaries and compendia" dates back to the beginning of the Church.

In this brief opening section, the *Directory* also wishes to make clear that the more extensive project of writing catechisms, teaching tools, for the worldwide Church, emerged in relation to two ecumenical (i.e. universal) Councils of the Church: the Council of Trent and the Second Vatican Council. Appropriately enough, universal catechisms followed universal Councils.[306] From the first of these issued the *Roman Catechism* and from the second, four hundred years later, the *Catechism of the Catholic Church*. The two catechisms, as one would expect, have much in common, not only in terms of the content of the faith but also in the structure and the pastoral notes for teaching that are given.[307]

## IDENTITY, AIM AND AUDIENCE

Following this brief historical note, the *Directory* then moves on to consider the identity, aim and audience of the *Catechism* and the points made here are closely related, of course, to those in the chapters in the *Directory* on the identity and aims of catechesis and the person of the catechist. The point of this short section is to tie the *Catechism* into those earlier points, establishing for the reader how the *Catechism* is a crucial instrument for serving the overall *aims of catechesis* and serving the *catechist*.

Regarding the aim and identity of the *Catechism*, then, the *Directory* sums up the *Catechism*'s distinctive character as one of offering "an organic summary of the heritage of faith". Gathered within its pages is a representation of the whole of

---

[305] *1 Corinthians* 15:3-5. The footnote to *DC* 58 provides us with examples of these early scriptural statements. For a detailed discussion on the development of the early creeds, cf. J.N.D. Kelly, *Early Christian Creeds*, 3rd ed., (London, Continuum, 2006).

[306] For the relationship of the *Catechism* to the Second Vatican Council cf. D. Bushman and L. Pollice, "The *Catechism* of Vatican II for the New Evangelisation", in P. Willey and S. Sollom (eds), *Speaking the Truth in Love* (Steubenville, Emmaus Academic, 2019) pp.3-24.

[307] Thus, to take two examples, the Scriptural quotations that lead the *Catechism* are found in the early pages of the *Roman Catechism*, and that earlier catechism also provides two of the pastoral directions found in the Prologue of the *CCC*, in nos.24 and 25.

Tradition in terms of the spirituality, theology and life of the Church. This heritage, this "cultural capital"[308] of Catholicism, is brought together between the covers of this text, which is therefore an immensely rich one.

The way in which this is achieved is in the form, the *Directory* says, of an "organic summary".[309] The phrase is worth a little attention. The immense gathering of Tradition is necessarily in the form of an abbreviation, with a focus upon fundamentals and essentials, thus yielding a *summary* account. Containing within itself other summaries of the faith[310] – such as creeds providing summaries of what is to be believed, and the Lord's Prayer, a summary of how we are to pray and petition our heavenly Father – the *Catechism* acts as a focused receptacle, concentrating the vision while at the same time introducing one to the immensity of the Mystery of the faith.

And the mode of this gathering has, above all, a concern for exhibiting the *organic unity* of the faith. The *Directory* wants to remind us here of the *unity* of the *Catechism*. While the *Catechism* can strike the reader at first as an unwieldy and challenging tome, the paragraphs in the *Catechism* are not presented here in its pages as 2865 separate statements of belief, for the reader to try to understand and order as best as he can. Rather, the *Catechism* presents the faith in such a way that the harmonious unity of every aspect of the faith with the central *kerygma* is highlighted, as members of a body around their head. The text takes pains to show how the living heart of the faith is present in each of the doctrines. It also helps the reader to understand the interrelationship of the items of faith with each other. The aim of the *Catechism*, then, is to support a "unitary act" of handing on the faith so that a corresponding unitary act of responding faith can be given to it. The *Catechism* is written so that the faith can be communicated as a "whole", as what the Church calls a *nexus mysteriorum*, with the revealed truths of the faith, the "mysteries", all bound together within the single Mystery of Christ.[311] When one is received as an adult into the Church one gives assent not to each and every teaching identified separately but states, "I believe and profess all that the holy Catholic Church believes, teaches, and proclaims to be revealed by God".[312] The capacity of an adult to make that profession, professing that single "all", is made possible when the delivery of the faith has made clear its organic unity.

The *Directory* uses a particular analogy to describe the gathering of the elements in Scripture and Tradition into this single organic unity. It speaks of the *Catechism's* "symphonic structure". As a great symphony, it says, the *Catechism* draws together

---

[308] For a discussion of how the *Catechism* draws together the riches of Catholic culture cf. T. Rowland, "The *Catechism* of the Catholic Church and the Culture of the Incarnation", in P. Willey and S. Sollom (eds), *Speaking the Truth in Love*, pp.219-230.

[309] *DC* 184.

[310] Cf. *CCC* 186, 2761.

[311] Cf. *CCC* 90.

[312] *Rite of Christian Initiation of Adults* 491.

Eastern and Western traditions, content and sources and the interrelationship of the virtues of faith, hope and love, all to manifest "the harmonious beauty that characterises Christian truth".[313] This image of a symphony, or a choir, is a particularly apt one, indicating as it does different instruments and voices sounding together to produce a form of beauty.

This symphonic image also links us to the question of who is to be the audience of the *Catechism*. For whom is the *Catechism* intended? The earlier *Roman Catechism* was composed to assist priests in their teaching, their homilies and their sacramental practice. This new *Catechism* is published "for the pastors and the faithful, and especially for those among them who have responsibility for the ministry of catechesis within the Church".[314] The audience is a wider one. Certainly it is for bishops, for those with ultimate responsibility for catechesis in the Church. But in the end it is for *all* those who need to catch the "echo" of Christ's teaching and hand it on faithfully. And this handing on is to be symphonic in that etymological sense of "sounding together".

The *Catechism*, then, is written to serve a harmonious transmission among its teachers and catechists: it has "as its first concern the unity of the Church in the one faith".[315] There is one Lord, one Church and one faith, and each catechist, whether ordained, religious, or lay, has as a first responsibility to echo this unity of truth in the one Body, gathered around Christ the Head. And if the "beautiful words" of the

---

[313] *DC* 191.
[314] *DC* 185.
[315] *DC* 186.

Head[316] are well-caught, if the echo is faithfully transmitted, it will be as an ample and symphonic sound, harmoniously uniting the different voices who attend to the many needs of distinctive inculturation. The *Directory* here quotes from the words of John Paul's Letter introducing the definitive edition of the *Catechism* – "the wondrous unity of the Christian mystery" will be linked to "the varied needs and conditions of those to whom this message is addressed".[317] To cite an earlier principle from the *Directory*, the individual catechist will successfully unite fidelity to God to a fidelity to the specific human persons being addressed.[318]

## SOURCES AND STRUCTURE OF THE *CATECHISM*

The theme of symphonic unity is continued in the discussion on sources. The *sources* of the *Catechism* are those we have already met in the *Directory* – the Sacred Scriptures, the liturgy, the Magisterium, the Fathers and Doctors of the Church, the beauty of her patrimony in the living examples of the saints and in her artistic heritage, the liturgies of East and West, and the vast riches of Catholic culture.[319] These, John Paul describes as the "living sources of the faith".[320] It is in and through an encounter with these that catechesis will be "renewed" because in these sources we encounter Christ in his beauty and his glory. The *Catechism* therefore presents itself as serving these sources, introducing them to the reader, providing avenues towards them, so that the catechist-reader can be immersed in them, learning directly from them. A comprehensive index of citations is provided as part of the official text of the *Catechism* for this reason, not simply as an aid to locating references, but as a witness to the sources of the faith from which catechesis draws its purest and truest life.

The *structure* of the *Catechism* is presented to us in both ecclesial and anthropological terms. The four parts of the *Catechism* take up the earliest reference we have to the form of Church life established by the apostles, which speaks of newly baptised believers devoting themselves steadfastly to the apostles' teaching, being united in prayer and fellowship and celebrating the "breaking of the bread".[321] The four parts of the *Catechism*, centred upon the Apostles' Creed, the sacraments, life in Christ and Christian prayer, mirror these fundamental components of early Church life. The structure of the *Catechism* is a kind of witness to the continuity of the faith and to God's faithfulness across the centuries in sustaining and upholding these "pillars of catechesis" and of the faith.

---

[316] *DC* 107.

[317] *DC* 186.

[318] *DC* 179.

[319] *DC* 90-109.

[320] St John Paul II's words from *Fidei Depositum* (1992) are cited in *DC* 187.

[321] *Acts* 2:42. The Greek, *proskarterountes*, indicates an unceasing attentiveness, an unremitting concentration. Cf. *DC* 189.

The structure of the *Catechism* is also, the *Directory* indicates, a witness to God's faithfulness to every human being who needs to receive formation in the truth, since these parts, or "pillars", correspond to "the fundamental dimensions of Christian life", providing a "paradigm for formation in the Christian life".[322] The life of each Christian consists in *believing* in the truth, *celebrating* the bountiful goodness of God and sharing this in *life together* with others, while *praying* to and contemplating the one who is the source of all Beauty. The *Catechism* is intended by the Church to be harnessed to support the catechetical formation of those dimensions, enabling an integrated and comprehensive formation of the person.

## THE THEOLOGICAL-CATECHETICAL SIGNIFICANCE OF THE *CATECHISM*

The final section on the *Catechism* draws together and reinforces the points that have been made. The *Catechism* exhibits the perennial principles of catechesis, the principles of God's and the Church's pedagogy in a way that every catechist can discover and appreciate. All of the criteria for presenting the faith that the *Directory* has expounded in chapter five are present in the *Catechism*: "Trinitarian and Christological centrality, the account of salvation history, the ecclesial nature of the message, the hierarchy of truths and the importance of beauty."[323] From the opening line onwards, the *Catechism* also "reserves a place of absolute prominence for God and for the work of grace."[324] It is from the *Catechism*, therefore, that the catechist learns not only the *content* of the faith but also the *craft* of catechesis.[325]

In this section, the *Directory* also turns to one further contribution the *Catechism* makes: its personal value to the catechist, not only as a resource for learning the faith and the tenets of the catechetical craft, but above all for feeding and maturing the catechist's life. The *Catechism* is a work of spiritual wisdom, which fosters through its language, its devotional appeal and its uniting of spirituality to doctrine, a deepening immersion of the reader in Christ's life, drawing the catechist closer to the divine Source of the craft and opening the catechist to the goodness and beauty of the God who is to be proclaimed and honoured in witness and teaching. The words of the *Catechism* are intended to lead to "the opening of the heart" and to support "the process of conversion and maturation". The knowledge presented in the *Catechism* is "not abstract"; it is intended to foster "encounter with Christ".[326]

This is a crucial point since the catechist is the one who *mediates* the faith to others. It matters, therefore, *how* the catechist practises his or her craft. And it matters *how*

---

[322] *DC* 189.
[323] *DC* 192.
[324] *DC* 192.
[325] For a discussion cf. P. de Cointet, B. Morgan and P. Willey, *The Catechism of the Catholic Church and the Craft of Catechesis* (San Francisco, Ignatius Press, 2008) pp.ix-xv, 1-24.
[326] *DC* 190.

the catechist reads the *Catechism*. And what makes the vital difference is whether or not the catechist has seen that on "page after page, we find that what is presented here is no theory, but an encounter with a Person who lives within the Church".[327] The *Catechism* must be approached first of all, therefore, as *a work of spirituality*, seeking the closer adherence and assent of the catechist to Christ and his teaching. The *Catechism* in fact emphasises this point to its readers in its Prologue, saying of itself:

> It seeks to help deepen understanding of faith. In this way it is oriented towards the maturing of that faith, its putting down roots in personal life, and its shining forth in personal conduct.[328]

The catechist who receives the teaching of the *Catechism* in this way, with the roots of the faith reaching deep into personal life, will be able to match the overarching principles of the faith to catechetical methods that are coherent with these principles, and be faithful to God's pedagogy while also being suited to the particular individuals – their age and capacities – to whom the catechist is ministering. The catechist who engages with the *Catechism* in this way will have placed him or herself under God's pedagogy, under his tutelage, and be able to discern the appropriate methodologies that can make room for his primacy in catechesis and faithfully enshrine his pedagogy. The next chapter, on methodology in catechesis, will take up this theme.

## THE *COMPENDIUM*

Before the *Directory* turns to the question of methodology it invites us briefly to consider the value of a sister companion to the *Catechism*, the *Compendium of the Catechism*. This single paragraph, no.193, refers us to the two texts that introduce the *Compendium*, to explain its purpose. The ultimate role of the *Compendium* is to assist a person in approaching the text of the *Catechism*, to discover the riches of the gathering of the faith in that volume. The *Compendium*, meanwhile, mirrors that content in a more concise form, one that is simple and accessible. It is intended as a helpful introduction to the faith that prepares one for the larger work of the *Catechism* that can deepen and mature what has been received in this smaller work.

Having said this, the *Directory* also notes the salient features of the *Compendium* itself that merit its presence in this *Directory* intended for the universal Church. While it is a stepping stone to the richer text of the *Catechism* it carries intrinsic value of its own. In the first place, its very *conciseness* allows one to behold "the entire panorama" of the faith very easily. It allows one to gain a vantage point for surveying the whole faith, grasping the beauty and grandeur of the Catholic landscape.

The *dialogical format* of the *Compendium* has its own value also. The style of the *Compendium* is that of "an imaginary dialogue between master and disciple, through a

---

[327] *DC* 190, quoting from Benedict XVI.
[328] *CCC* 23.

series of incisive questions that invite the reader to go deeper in discovering ever new aspects of his faith". We have a representation here of that "laboratory of dialogue" which the *Directory* proposes, together with an image of accompaniment in the faith, modelling the formation of personal disciples in the faith as the mentor figure draws the disciple more and more deeply into the life of Christ.[329]

A third feature of the *Compendium* is the presence of fourteen *images* introducing and often providing artistic synthesis to the different divisions of the *Compendium*. The glorious apse of San Clemente, for example, introduces the Creed, representing in mosaic the unity of faith gathered around the figure of Christ on the Cross, with the apostles, symbolised by doves after the descent of the Holy Spirit at Pentecost, settled in the beams of the Cross which is held by the hand of the Father. The sources of the faith, meanwhile, are represented by streams, all contributing to a vibrant sense of the life of the Church depicted as a vine.

This use of images (also present in the *Catechism* to introduce each of the four parts) is not merely decorative but both catechetical – communicating the mysteries of the faith "in the splendour of colour and in the perfection of beauty"[330]– and also a reminder of the importance of the *via pulchritudinis*, the way of beauty, in catechesis.[331]

Finally, the *Compendium* allows the catechist to use its content for *memorisation* of the faith: in addition to the basic text, the *Compendium* supplies prayers and creedal statements to assist in this regard. This is a topic of importance that will be taken up, also, in the following chapter.

## QUESTIONS FOR REFLECTION

1   Do I regularly read the *Catechism*?
  • How do I use it to prepare for my catechetical ministry?
2   How might I build the reading of the *Catechism* more fully into my life?

---

[329] Cf. *DC* 53-54, 135c.
[330] *Introduction of Cardinal Joseph Ratzinger to the Compendium of the Catechism of the Catholic Church*, 20th March 2005, 5.
[331] We can recall the section *DC* 106-109. It is a theme that will be taken up again in the following chapter, 209-212.

# A Prayer for Catechists

HEAVENLY FATHER,
You are the unceasing giver who always provides
  for your Church.
Thank you for the gift of the *Catechism*,
A sure reference point where we can seek and find
  your truths,
A place for being drawn closer to you,
to learn to love you in your Mystery,
And a rich source for learning the craft of catechesis.
Give us always thankful and trusting hearts
Open to learn from the Church,
our mother and teacher.
We ask this in the name of your Son
And our teacher, Jesus Christ.
Amen.

# CHAPTER VII:

# Methodology in Catechesis

### THE RELATIONSHIP BETWEEN CONTENT AND METHOD (Paragraphs 194-196)

A false dichotomy that continues to persist in catechesis is presented by those who would pit content against methodology, placing emphasis on one above the other. These two variables are not opposite ends of the same continuum; they are inextricably intertwined. If we do not hand on the faith both authentically and comprehensively, we are not catechists, for the very word "catechesis" means "to echo" (from the Greek words *kata* [back] and *eche* [sound]). On the other hand, if we do not use methods that speak effectively to learners, we have not transmitted the message at all. In fact, if we lack knowledge about the level of understanding of our learners and are using methodologies that are developmentally inappropriate, we might inadvertently transmit a *mis*understanding of the faith.[332]

Like the catechetical documents that preceded it, the *Directory for Catechesis* appropriately presents content and method as two variables, closely related, and both essential. The present directory calls this perspective "a matter of living out fidelity to God and humanity."[333] The point is made here that the method must fit the content, which requires careful reflection on both the nature of the message and the needs of the community and individuals concerned. Also affirmed in this chapter is that

---

[332] For a more extensive discussion of this issue of "heresy by methodology," cf. P. Willey & S. Sollom (eds), *Speaking the Truth in Love: the Catechism and the New Evangelisation*, pp. 429-430.
[333] *DC* 194.

there is no one method for teaching the faith. In paragraph 195 the *Directory* calls the plurality of methods "a sign of life and richness," a nod to the 1997 *General Directory for Catechesis*, which, quoting *Catechesi Tradendae*, states, "the 'variety of methods is a sign of life and richness,' as well as a demonstration of respect for those to whom catechesis is addressed."[334] In other words, those individuals and groups being formed in the catechetical process will experience the vitality and depth of the Gospel message in part through the variety of ways in which we present it. Catechists who are tethered inflexibly to one method risk presenting a one-dimensional message that is unengaging, shallow, and unrepresentative of the richness and relevance of God's truths for today.

In this section of the *Directory*, we are also reminded of the role of grace in catechesis. This is both an admonition and a reassurance for the catechist. Whether or not our learners hear and respond to a truth of the faith is not solely dependent on whether we use the right methods. It is not all up to us, and *thank God* it's not all up to us. Here we are reminded of what is said in Sacred Scripture: "so shall my word be that goes out from my mouth; it shall not return to me empty, but it shall accomplish that which I purpose, and succeed in the thing for which I sent it."[335]

A disappointing aspect of the recent history of secular general education is the tendency to adopt new approaches without careful discernment. New teaching methodologies have at times become widespread trends before we have had an opportunity to evaluate their results. As a consequence, particular cohorts of learners have had lower levels of achievement than previous and future students in particular subject areas, such as maths or reading, simply because it was fashionable in their formative years to teach these subjects in a new and different way. While the new directory encourages creativity in the selection of methods and openness to new approaches, we are also cautioned to discern carefully the methods we use, and to appropriately evaluate their effectiveness.[336]

## HUMAN EXPERIENCE (Paragraphs 197-200)

A contentious issue in catechesis in the last few decades has been the place of human experience in catechesis. Questions have arisen regarding whether human experience should be the beginning or end point of catechesis (inductive or deductive methodology), and various sides have accused one another of placing too much – or too little – emphasis on experience at the expense of orthodoxy, or vice-versa. Again, we would do well here to look for guidance to key catechetical documents from the Magisterium of the Church. Particularly in the decades following the Second Vatican

---

[334] *GDC* 148.
[335] *Isaiah* 55:11 (NRSV-CE).
[336] *DC* 196.

Council, the Church has affirmed the importance of human experience in catechesis and given guidance to catechists regarding its proper role in the process of formation. In his masterwork on catechesis, St John Paul II writes,

> Authentic catechesis is always an orderly and systematic initiation into the revelation that God has given of himself to humanity in Christ Jesus, a revelation stored in the depths of the Church's memory and in Sacred Scripture, and constantly communicated from one generation to the next by a living, active *traditio*. This revelation is not however isolated from life or artificially juxtaposed to it. It is concerned with the ultimate meaning of life and it illumines the whole of life with the light of the Gospel, to inspire it or to question it.[337]

The *Directory for Catechesis* affirms the sentiments of this great catechetical saint, calling human experience "integral to catechesis...because it is not only the place in which the word of God is proclaimed but also the space in which God speaks."[338] This section of the *Directory* sets the stage for accompaniment of the learner by reminding those of us in catechetical ministry of God's actions in the life of each individual and our need to be open to God's presence there, which, the *Directory* asserts, helps the catechist to see the process of formation as a reciprocal and dialogical one.

The *Directory* cites Jesus's own ministry as an example of the use of human experience in transmission of the faith,[339] as Jesus meets people in the everyday situations of their lives, and he teaches using parables that in many ways would have been, for the people of his time and culture, stories about everyday people and situations.[340] However, these stories held a deeper meaning, as they helped the followers of Jesus to understand God's message to them and his plan for their lives. The *Directory* points out that when we follow the example of Jesus in our work as catechists, we also will help people "illuminate and interpret" their life experiences "in the light of the Gospel."[341] The secularisation of Western societies, especially, has led to a compartmentalisation of faith – an artificial separation between body, mind and spirit and between faith and everyday life. A Catholic worldview, on the other hand, presents the human person as an integrity of body, mind and spirit, in which each aspect of the human person is interrelated. This understanding naturally presents one's relationship with God as interwoven with one's life experiences. This is the only way that the seeds of the Gospel can take root and bear fruit, for "faith by itself, if it has no works, is dead."[342]

---

[337] *CT* 22.
[338] *DC* 197.
[339] *DC* 198.
[340] *DC* 200.
[341] *DC* 199.
[342] *James* 2:17 (NRSV-CE).

## MEMORY (Paragraphs 201-203)

In his Apostolic Exhortation, *Catechesi Tradendae*, St John Paul II writes, "The blossoms, if we may call them that, of faith and piety do not grow in the desert places of a memory-less catechesis."[343] He makes it clear in this seminal work on catechesis that he is referring not simply to memorisation (although this is included), but also to memory in the sense that we are keepers of a tradition of faith that is handed down through the generations.

In the Jewish tradition, memorialising an event of salvation history brought that event, in a certain sense, to the present moment. Thus, in the Passover Seder, the question is asked "Why *is this* night different from all other nights?" (vs. "Why *was that* night different from all other nights?"). This tradition of bringing the past into the present through memorial prefigures the celebration of the Eucharist itself. The present *Directory* cites this tradition of memorial in the Judeo-Christian tradition,[344] as well as the tradition of memorisation in Church history[345] in order to convey, as St John Paul II did, the importance of memory in catechesis. Here again, it is important not to fall into a false dichotomy (this time of orthodoxy vs. orthopraxis). Faith that does not change one's daily life is not faith at all (cf. *James* 2:17); however, it is equally true that one cannot live a faith that one does not know. A knowledge of the faith, committed to memory, is necessary for mature Christian living, and so is an understanding of how to apply that faith to one's decision, actions, and worldview.

The *Directory* makes it clear that articles of faith not just be memorised, but also understood, "internalised" and lived, and this will be more likely when we consider memorisation "in relationship with other elements of the catechetical process, like relationship, dialogue, reflection, silence and accompaniment."[346]

## LANGUAGE (Paragraphs 204-217)

The *Directory* points out that catechesis not only adapts to the language of individuals based on developmental level, culture, and other variables, but also helps to transmit a common language of faith that shapes our understanding of the sacred.[347] This common language is essential not only to bringing unity to the Church, but is also vital to its survival. Sociologists note that when the language of a culture dies, the culture itself fragments and dies shortly thereafter. This is precisely because language is so integral to our cultural identity. The same is true for our identity as Catholics. Historically, the primary languages of the Church have been biblical, symbolic-

---

[343] *CT* 55; cf. *DC* 202.
[344] *DC* 201.
[345] *DC* 202.
[346] *DC* 203.
[347] *DC* 204.

liturgical, doctrinal, and performative.[348] The Church also "creatively adopts", the *Directory* asserts, the language of various cultures.[349] This section of the *Directory* goes on to discuss three different cultural expressions of language that are especially relevant to our time – narrative language, the language of art, and digital languages and tools.

## Narrative and Autobiographic Language

The *Directory* points out how various fields of study have highlighted the importance of narration for organising and reflecting on our experiences and discusses how narrative has been used in the handing on of the story of salvation history.[350] Indeed, story, in part because it involves so many aspects of our nature – intellect, emotions, and spirit – has been a primary way in which both the Jewish and Christian faiths have been handed down across the generations. And the telling of this story, the *Directory* points out, has continued to include the history of the Church through the generations, up to the present time. This story includes not just the community, but each member individually.[351] Therefore, narration is useful not only for understanding the events of salvation history but also the story of the Church through the ages as well as one's own journey of faith and role in the family of God.

---

348 *DC* 205.
349 *DC* 206.
350 *DC* 207.
351 *DC* 208.

## The Language of Art

Dr. Jem Sullivan writes, "We believe that in Christ Jesus, God is decisively revealed in human history. Now, matter really matters. Images of beauty that transform matter, and make visible the invisible mystery of God, are now an essential part of Christian worship. As Pope Benedict notes in *The Spirit of the Liturgy*, 'The complete absence of images is incompatible with faith in the Incarnation of God.'"[352] The *Directory for Catechesis* speaks of the rich history of images in our faith and the value of those images in handing on Catholic teaching.[353] In recent years, with the advent of digital media (particularly social media platforms), visual imagery has only increased in importance with respect to telling a story in a compelling and effective manner. Multisensory methodology, including visual imagery, is also important for the many ways in which people learn (some are primarily auditory learners, while others prefer visual or tactile learning materials). Diversity of presentation helps a greater percentage of one's audience to be engaged. It is also critical for diverse learning needs. For example, individuals with reading language disabilities depend heavily on visual imagery for understanding.

Also discussed is the value of music in our faith, which the *Directory* calls "a precious asset for evangelisation."[354] Music has a vital role in our liturgy, and the *Directory* point out that doctrinally rich songs assist in not only stimulating the intellect but also touching the heart, resulting in a message that "more easily enters the mind and impresses itself in a deeper way on people's hearts".[355]

The arts – visual arts, music, and others like literature, cinema and theater, which are also mentioned in this section of the *Directory*, help catechists make use of beauty – one of the three transcendental properties of being (truth, beauty and goodness) to which philosophers and theologians have pointed throughout history that have the ability to raise our awareness towards something bigger than ourselves.[356] The poison of relativism has permeated so much of the modern world, especially in Western societies, that many individuals are sceptical that objective truth can even exist. An initial encounter with the Gospel, for those individuals, might need to come in the form of either goodness or beauty.

---

[352] *Catechist's Companion to the Compendium of the Catholic Church,* p. 13; cf. Joseph Ratzinger, *The Spirit of the Liturgy* (San Francisco, Ignatius Press, 2000).

[353] *DC* 209-210.

[354] *DC* 211.

[355] *DC* 211.

[356] The *Directory for Catechesis* makes direct reference to the three transcendentals in this passage from paragraph 172: "The word of God, mediated by catechesis, illuminates human life, conferring its deepest meaning upon it and accompanying human beings on the paths of the beautiful, the true, and the good."

## Digital Languages and Tools

The *Directory for Catechesis* discusses the profound changes in recent decades in the area of communication, particularly with regard to digital technologies. The cultural sea change that has resulted from rapid developments in the digital world, and their influence on culture as a whole, are discussed in more detail in chapter ten of the *Directory* (particularly paragraphs 365-372). In the present chapter, digital technologies are discussed in the context of methodology. Specifically, the point is made that without some use of digital technology in catechesis we risk appearing irrelevant or "insignificant to many people."[357] In contrast to methodologies that assume a more one-way communication from catechist to learner, many digital technologies (especially social media platforms) allow for more interaction between learners and dialogue between the catechist and the individuals in formation.[358] This is conducive to the dialogical nature of accompaniment emphasised in the *Directory* as a whole.

The *Directory* emphasises the importance of reaching people in the modern world with tools they are accustomed to using in other learning environments.[359] In addition, we are warned about the profound influence the digital world can make, especially on younger generations, with regard to identity and emotional regulation, and cautioned that the virtual world cannot replace real life interactions, especially in our Catholic faith.[360]

## THE GROUP (Paragraphs 218-220)

One of the common threads that run through the *Directory for Catechesis* is the idea that the Christian community is both a privileged place of formation and a catechist. This theme is highlighted again here in the chapter on methodology, which calls the Christian community "the primary agent of catechesis."[361] It is part of our human nature that we, created as social beings, want and need to be with one another and have a desire to belong. The Christian community offers a place where everyone belongs, and when we are open to the Holy Spirit, we grow in our unity and our love for one another. The new directory speaks of the formative power of the group dynamic for each individual person, and calls the experience of the group "fertile soil for welcoming and sharing the message of salvation."[362]

We are encouraged, in this section of the *Directory*, to use research from the human sciences, such as education and psychology, to help us better understand

---

[357] *DC* 213.
[358] *DC* 214, 215.
[359] *DC* 216.
[360] *DC* 217; cf. *Directory for Catechesis*, 361, 370.
[361] *DC* 218.
[362] *DC* 219.

group dynamics and educational processes in group settings.[363] In this way, we can better ensure that we capitalise on the advantages of a community experience of catechesis. In addition, we are reminded that "every group dynamic has its summit in the Sunday assembly", where the group is prepared to serve and bear witness in the larger world[364] – a truth that can help us guard against cliquishness or the tendency to find our identity in something other than our common identity as daughters and sons of God and members of his Church.

## SPACE

The final portion of this chapter on methodology in the *Directory for Catechesis* focuses on the importance of space, both in our Catholic tradition and in catechesis in particular.[365] The importance of creating spaces that are intentional and welcoming is discussed, and we are cautioned against using "spaces patterned after school buildings" without adapting them with reflection on the goals and meaning of the catechetical process.[366] We are challenged here to consider how the specific tasks of catechesis lend themselves to different seating arrangements, for example, or a room that is arranged to focus on a sacred space that includes icons and other sacred

---

[363] *DC* 220.
[364] *DC* 220.
[365] *DC* 221.
[366] *DC* 222.

objects. Because the community experience of formation should point us to the larger community experience of the Sunday Mass, catechists might wish to consider incorporating into these sacred spaces the colors of the liturgical year and objects that connect with timely feasts in the Church calendar.

A final point in this section concerns the various environments we might wish to consider for catechesis, given our call to take the Gospel message out into the world in the places where people are already gathering. Advantages of this, according to the *Directory*, include the disarming nature of familiar settings and more visible connections between catechesis and everyday life.[367]

## QUESTIONS FOR REFLECTION

1   In which of the methods discussed in this chapter do you feel most proficient?
    - How might you seek out additional training in the methods that come less naturally to you?

2   The end of this chapter challenges us to see the space we use for catechesis as part of our methodology. How might you be more intentional in arranging the space for your catechetical sessions?

---

[367] *DC* 223.

# A Prayer for Catechists

HEAVENLY FATHER,

You reveal yourself to us in a variety of ways.

Grant that I might be faithful to you and to humanity

by handing on your truth using a variety of methods.

Fill me with your Holy Spirit,

that I might be creative in my approach

so everyone might hear your Word.

We ask this in the name of Christ Jesus.

Amen.

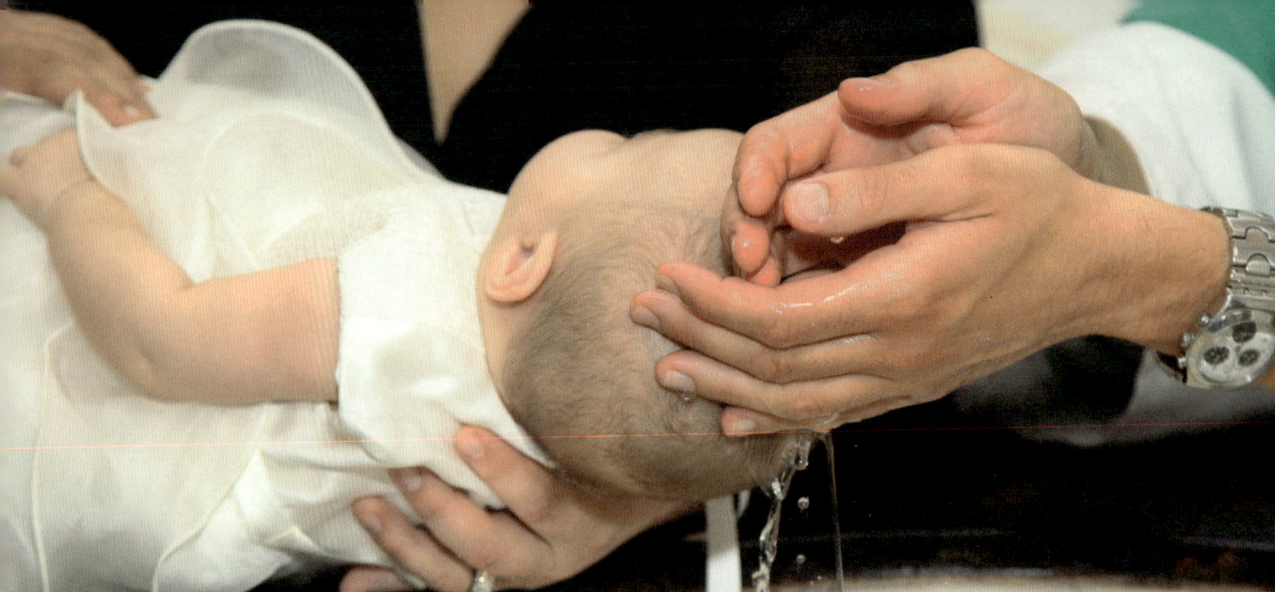

## CHAPTER VIII:

# Catechesis in the Lives of Persons

C hapter eight of the *Directory* begins by emphasising the need for catechesis to consider the particular situation of each human being, "marked by psychological, social, cultural and religious dynamics."[368] The *Directory* describes the relationship between faith and development, stating, "faith is not a linear process, and it participates in the development of the person, and this in turn influences the journey of faith."[369] These points are made to explain the need to adapt catechesis based on the ages, stages of life, and particular situations of those being catechised.[370] Doing this well necessarily involves using what we know from the human sciences, like education and psychology, about how people grow, and how their needs and understanding change as a consequence of that growth.

### CATECHESIS AND THE FAMILY (Paragraphs 226-235)

The family is central to our Catholic Faith. God reveals himself as a "family" – Father, Son and Holy Spirit – a communion of persons.[371] God created us, male and female, in his image and likeness. We are created to be in communion with one another. Jesus reveals God as a Father who loves and cares for his children. The Church is revealed to us as a family into which we are adopted by God and become brothers and sisters

---

[368] *DC* 224.
[369] *DC* 224.
[370] *DC* 224.
[371] *Genesis* 1:26-27; *CCC* 2205.

to one another.[372] Jesus's relationship with the Church is presented in Scripture as a marriage, with Jesus as the Groom and the Church his Bride.

The family also has a privileged place in catechesis. The *Catechism* states that "parents receive the responsibility of evangelising their children" and calls them the "first heralds" of the faith.[373] The family is also called "domestic church"—the church of the home.[374] Catechesis in the parish or Catholic school can give structure and support to faith formation in the home. Parish and school catechesis are systematic and comprehensive, while the formation that parents provide in the home is more organic and focused on particular occasions in the life of the family. Parents play an indispensable role in helping the faith come alive for their children. The family is the first place where each of us is called to live the faith that we have received.

The *Directory* devotes several paragraphs to the discussion of catechesis and the family. In the introduction to this section, the Church is called a "family of families," and the *Directory* echoes a well-known quote on the family by St John Paul II, saying "The future of persons and the human and ecclesial communities depends to a large extent on the family, the basic cell of society."[375]

## Areas of Family Catechesis

The *Directory for Catechesis* discuss three "areas of family catechesis": "catechesis *in* the family", "catechesis *with* the family", and the "catechesis *of* the family."[376] The first area, catechesis in the family, refers to the unique ability of the family to transmit the faith in "simple and spontaneous" ways through the routines and events in everyday life.[377] The family can, and should, be a context in which children learn to pray, to make good choices, and to treat others with love and respect. This happens primarily through the witness of parents in the home.[378]

*Catechesis with the family* refers to the reciprocal relationship between the family and the Church community – a "family of families."[379] The family enfleshes the message of faith, making it visible in everyday life, and the community provides "an explicit key for using faith to reinterpret its experience."[380] Important aspects of this contribution of the community include proclaiming the *kerygma*, the core of the Gospel message to

---

[372] *Galatians* 4:4-5.
[373] *CCC* 2225.
[374] *CCC* 2224.
[375] Cf. Homily of St John Paul II (Perth, Australia, 30th November 1986): Par. 4 (*http://www.vatican.va/content/john-paul-ii/en/homilies/1986/documents/hf_jp-ii_hom_19861130_perth-australia.html*).
[376] *DC* 227-231 (italics added).
[377] *DC* 227.
[378] *DC* cf. *GDC* 255.
[379] *DC* 229.
[380] *DC* 229.

families, as well as assisting families in the tasks that are part of its mission: transmitting life, educating their children, and fostering authentic spirituality.[381]

*The catechesis of the family* includes "the specific contribution that Christian families make...to the various journeys of faith that the community proposes."[382] This refers to the missionary activity of the family, both the way in which parents hand on the faith to their children, and the way the family spreads the faith through their witness to the world around them.

## Pastoral Guidelines

The *Directory* offers specific guidelines for catechesis of the family in six areas:

    a. *Preparation for marriage*, which the *Directory* proposes should be inspired by the catechumenate and include a "renewed proclamation of the *kerygma*."[383]

    b. *The catechesis of young married couples*, which the *Directory* suggests should be presented in mystagogic form, to assist couples in better understanding what they have received and living out the Sacrament of Matrimony.[384]

    c. *The catechesis of persons who are asking to have their children baptised*, which the *Directory* states should "welcome, listen to, and understand the reason for the parents' request, and provide an appropriate pathway for them to reawaken the grace of the gift of faith that they have received."[385]

    d. *The catechesis of parents whose children are making the journey of Christian initiation*, which the *Directory* points out for some parents will be an opportunity to reawaken their faith, and of others an occasion for the first proclamation of the faith.

    e. *Intergenerational catechesis*, which, inspired by the early Church, facilitates exchange between the generations, using the liturgical year as a roadmap.[386]

    f. *Catechesis in groups of spouses and in groups of families*, carried out by married couples, assists families in developing "a conjugal and family spirituality capable of restoring strength and vitality to married life, rediscovering the spousal dimension of the covenant between God and humanity, and the role of the family in building the kingdom of God."[387]

---

[381] *DC* 230.
[382] *DC* 231.
[383] *DC* 232; cf. *AL*, 207.
[384] *DC* 232.
[385] *DC* 232.
[386] *DC* 232.
[387] *DC* 232.

## New Family Scenarios

The final portion of the section in the *Directory* on catechesis and the family discusses the reality of the breakdown of the family in contemporary society and the resulting number of divorced persons, blended families, and other family situations that pastoral leaders might view as "irregular". Here, the *Directory* emphasises the need to welcome and include these families and accompany them in discovering God's plan for their lives and growing in their relationship with Christ and his Church.[388]

## CATECHESIS WITH CHILDREN AND TEENAGERS (Paragraphs 236-243)

The *Directory* reflects on the importance of helping children "to perceive and to develop the sense of God."[389] Children, the *Directory* asserts, have a natural capacity to relate to God and to pose existential questions even when their parents are not religious. The *Directory* encourages those responsible for catechesis of children to make use of knowledge from human sciences such as education, psychology and sociology in order to lead them more effectively, and also reflects on how geographical and cultural differences can lead to diverse needs in the catechesis of children and adolescents. Mentioned briefly here (and discussed at more length in paragraphs 365-372) are the unique characteristics of *digital natives*, those members of the younger generations who have grown up in a highly technological environment.[390] Also discussed are the

---

[388] *DC* 233-235.
[389] *DC* 236.
[390] *DC* 237.

unique needs of children whose lives have been affected by poverty, violence, and family discord or instability.[391]

In the sections that follow, the *Directory* discusses the needs of various ages of children, based on their developmental characteristics. The section on *early childhood* discusses this period of life as a critical time in which openness to God is either encouraged and fostered or discouraged. There is evidence in the human sciences, particularly child psychology and pediatric neuropsychiatry, to support this idea as well.[392] In the pre-school years, the parts of the brain that are responsible for attachment and relationship are growing at their most rapid pace of growth. A pre-school programme of religious education that introduces children to Jesus as both God and friend, and introduces the parish church as a community of friends and an extended family, would help to develop an attachment to the faith at exactly the time that the attachment mechanisms in the brain are growing most rapidly. It is also important to engage the family and support them in raising their children in faith during these years. The first few years of a child's life are an important time as families change and realign many aspects of their lives to accommodate this new family member. These changes influence the family's social life, as couples often go from spending time primarily with people who do not have children to interacting most often with other couples with young children. Schedules and priorities also change due to the responsibilities of parenthood.

This family restructuring is an important opportunity for evangelisation, as during this period especially the parish can become a critically important part of the support structures that families craft for themselves. An ideal time to engage with the family is in the process of preparation for the Sacrament of Baptism – a process which is too often reduced to a half-day session that focuses merely on the words and movements of the rite itself, rather than preparation of the parents to live out the vows they are making on behalf of their child. What if parishes were to partner with parents at the time of Baptism – to place the community at the side of parents and continue walking with them?

Following the section on early childhood, this chapter of the *Directory* shifts its focus to middle childhood (ages 6-10).[393] This is the period, the *Directory* states, when according to tradition "the Christian initiation begun with Baptism is completed in the parish."[394] The *Directory* once again points to the baptismal catechumenate as inspiration for catechesis during this period, and rightly so, since this period is

---

[391] *DC* 238.
[392] White, J.D., 'Developmentally Responsive Catechesis and the *Catechism*'. In P. Willey and S. Sollom (eds), *Speaking the Truth in Love: The Catechism and the New Evangelisation* (Steubenville, Ohio, Emmaus Academic, 2020) pp. 429-440.
[393] *DC* 240.
[394] *DC* 240.

concerned with initiation into all aspects of the Christian life, reinforced by the witness of the Christian community.[395] The *Directory* speaks about the intellectual, affective and relational growth that coincides with the child's entry into the larger community,[396] and given the emphasis on understanding the physiognomy of children and its relationship to catechesis,[397] it makes sense here to discuss in some detail what the educational and social sciences have taught us about the development of children in this age group and to connect these findings to both a proposed itinerary of catechetical formation and catechetical methodology in this period of life.

Age six. Because this is the beginning of formal religious education for many children, and because the aim of catechesis is "communion and intimacy with Jesus Christ" (*GDC*, 80), it is logical to concentrate first grade catechesis around the person of Jesus. Six-year-olds are just beginning to move beyond the developmental self-focus of the pre-school years, so an introduction to relationship with Jesus and the Church community is appropriate. Children this age are beginning to move into a cognitive stage of rule-based thinking, so this is a great opportunity to provide them with the basic teachings of the faith. In the Judeo-Christian tradition, these basic teachings are often communicated in the form of stories. Interactive storytelling techniques involving visuals, three dimensional props, and acting out the story can be especially engaging activities for children this age.

Age seven. Children this age have usually entered into the Piagetian cognitive stage of "concrete operations".[398] They understand cause and effect and know the world works according to rules. Therefore, this is a great time to introduce God's rules and guidelines for living. Because they have reached the age of reason, seven-year-olds are better able to understand that the Eucharist is not ordinary bread and wine, because Jesus said it was his Body and Blood. Seven-year-olds are concrete thinkers and need many hands-on activities and practical explanations. Our approach to teaching the sacraments should be step-by-step and very concrete. This is a good time to learn the steps of the rites, parts of the Mass, and basics of what the Church teachers about the sacraments.

Age eight. Children this age have often entered what social/developmental theorist Harry Stack Sullivan called the "chumship stage," when same-age peers become very important and children often have "best friends".[399] For this reason, it is an ideal time to concentrate on the parish community. Eight-year-olds are more aware of the larger

---

[395] *DC* 242.

[396] *DC* 241.

[397] *DC* 237.

[398] For a more detailed discussion about Piaget's stages of cognitive development, cf. Piaget, J. in Gruber, H.E.; Voneche, J.J. (eds), *The Essential Piaget* (New York, Basic Books, 1977).

[399] Sullivan, Harry Stack, *The Interpersonal Theory of Psychiatry* (New York, W.W. Norton & Company, 1953).

world, so this is a good time to talk about the larger worldwide Church and how it is organised. The sense of the larger community makes an ideal time for eight-year-olds to do some learning in pairs or co-operative groups. To do this effectively, catechists should make sure the tasks are well defined, that each participant has a unique role, and that time limits and transition times are given.

Ages nine to ten. Children this age are beginning to internalise standards of behaviour. Their consciences are growing quickly, and they are gaining a sense of "right" and "wrong" that goes beyond just what might bring them punishments or rewards. This is a great time to work with them on what it means to be disciples of Jesus. Nine- and ten-year-olds are good at using their concrete reasoning skills, but they still do not have a firm grasp on hypothetical reasoning. This means they have difficulty imagining things or situations they haven't experienced. Role playing or acting out making good choices in a moral dilemma will be especially effective, since all of us are more likely to do the things that we practise.

## CATECHESIS IN THE REALM OF YOUNG PEOPLE (paragraphs 244-256)

### Catechesis with Pre-adolescents

Although older children and teens are mentioned briefly in the previous section, this section of the chapter discusses these age groups in more detail. Echoing Pope Francis's Apostolic Exhortation to young people, *Christus Vivit*, the *Directory* highlights the fresh perspective, optimism and energy that are characteristic of youth.[400] The *Directory* again emphasises the role of the whole community in the formation of young people, and compares this role to the Gospel account of Jesus meeting his disciples on the road to Emmaus, "his walking with them, dialoguing, accompanying, helping to open their eyes."[401] A general consideration offered in this section is that knowledge of social media and the virtual world are essential if we wish to speak in the language of young people today.[402]

Pre-adolescence is defined by the *Directory* as the ages from ten to fourteen and is described as a passage between the safety of the childhood years into the new an unfamiliar world of adolescence – a transition marked by both excitement and possible anxiety or confusion.[403] The *Directory* points out that this is a time of rapid physical and emotional growth, and also a time in which the young person's concepts of God and faith are "refashioned". The importance of attending to information from the human sciences is again reiterated here.

---

[400] *DC* 244, cf. *ChV* 18.
[401] *DC* 244.
[402] *DC* 245.
[403] *DC* 246.

Ten-year-olds are growing in their ability to understand symbols and signs. This makes this age an ideal time to take a deeper look at the sacraments and rites of the Church. As children turn eleven, they are often entering a stage of identity development in which they begin to consider seriously who they will be when they are older. Hence this age an important time for learning about vocations in general and the sacraments at the service of Holy Communion in particular. It is helpful to ask children this age to consider what God's plan for their life might be, and encourage them to seek that plan in the talents and opportunities God has given them.

Twelve-year-olds are growing in their ability to think abstractly and have made great strides in reading and writing ability. This makes this age an ideal time to study Sacred Scripture and begin to connect the events of salvation history. The use of Bible timelines can assist children with this. Children this age are also becoming young adolescents, so this is an important time to strengthen Catholic identity through study of our faith ancestors and basic doctrines. Studying the saints and how they articulated and defended the Catholic faith can be helpful. As the *Directory* instructs us, it is helpful to use the message of the *kerygma* "to pay special attention to the Lord Jesus as a brother who loves, as a friend who helps one be at one's best in relationships, does not judge, is faithful, values skills and dreams, bringing one's desires for beauty and goodness to fulfilment."[404]

The continued physical growth at the ages of thirteen and fourteen years brings identity issues and questions. Young people this age are often highly insecure and

---

[404] *DC 247.*

self-conscious. They are looking for both a reassurance that they are "normal" and a sense of belonging with others. They also want to see that the faith is relevant to them. If they cannot make connections between their faith and their everyday lives, they might question the importance of what they are learning in a catechetical setting. Concentrating on discipleship – following Jesus – can address the identity issues at this stage, while continued focus on the Church as community (and how they can actively participate in the Church) can help young people this age feel a sense of belonging. The *Directory* recommends that catechesis at this age "create a context of meaningful group relationships" and "take seriously the doubts and anxieties of the pre-adolescent, acting as a discreet but present companion."[405]

## Catechesis with Adolescents

In discussion of the adolescent years, defined here as the ages from fourteen to twenty-one, the *Directory* touches on the tension during these years between desiring independence and autonomy on the one hand and the fear of separating from the family and launching into adult life on the other.[406] During these years, young people might have many questions about their identity and purpose. Throughout the teen years and into early adulthood, people commonly ask themselves such questions as, "Who am I?", "Why am I here?" and "What will my future hold?" As Catholics, we believe that our faith has the only complete and fully satisfying answers to these existential questions, so as catechists we have an opportunity to share a great gift

---

[405] *DC* 247.
[406] *DC* 248.

with adolescent learners – the gift of the meaning, purpose and identity they can find in Jesus Christ and his Church.

Young people in these adolescent years might also question or even challenge Catholic teachings as they are presented. This occurs for a couple of different reasons. First, many (if not most) teens we encounter have been educated not only by the curriculum chosen by their parish or school, but also by the curriculum of popular culture, which is increasingly at odds with Catholic teaching. Through social media, music, television, advertising, peer interactions, and other sources, adolescents have been presented with ideas that might sound sensible to them, but are often based on fallacious ideas and systems of moral decision making. From hedonism ("If it feels good, do it") to individualism ("What's in it for me?") to relativism ("There is no objective right or wrong; live your personal truth"), there are many ideas competing for the minds and souls of our young people. It's important that catechists and others who form adolescents are patient, realising that evangelisation must precede catechesis. In a society that is often far from the will of God, we must prepare the soil before God's Word can take root and grow.

A second reason for the sometimes contentious questions we hear from teens in catechetical settings is that the adolescent years are a time of individuation. Adolescents are becoming more and more independent as they prepare for the time in which they will leave home to make lives and families of their own. This is a normal developmental process, for without some individuation from the family, especially in the later teen years, young adults would feel lost and incapable of making their way in the world. During the adolescent years, it sometimes seems that young people go from trusting everything adults say to questioning everything they are told. They eventually find a middle ground, where they have formed their own opinions and have set their own goals, but have also taken important lessons and wisdom of those who came before them.

It is axiomatic that faith is one thing we certainly want our young people to carry with them into their adult lives. Questioning and struggling with the faith is an important way that some adolescents eventually make the faith their own, such that they are no longer Catholic simply because their parents and family are Catholic, but because they have come to see the faith as true and personally meaningful. To this end, it would benefit adolescents to have adults accompanying and guiding them in this process, as the *Directory for Catechesis* recommends. In their research on the stability of faith in the transition from adolescence to adulthood, the Fuller Youth Institute has proposed that children and teens are most likely to remain committed to their faith during this transitional period if they have a meaningful relationship with at least five adults who are intentionally living out their faith; this has been called the "5:1 ratio".[407]

---

[407] *fulleryouthinstitute.org/articles/moving-away-from-the-kid-table* (For more information on the scope and methodology of the research, cf. *fulleryouthinstitute.org/stickyfaith/research*.)

## Catechesis with Young People

Young adults are discussed in the following section, which highlights the diverse situations of people in this age group around the world, including insecurity due to a lack of jobs, migration and resulting isolation, and lack of hope in parts of the world where the realities of adult life fall short of interests and expectations.[408] The *Directory* also refers to variety in the religious experiences of young adults, from those who have turned away from the Church for various reasons, to those who are actively involved in Catholic practice, both in the parish and in the community.[409]

The *Directory* calls for catechesis with young adults to be "redefined by the features of" a "pastoral style" that includes several components mentioned in Pope Francis's Apostolic Exhortation, *Christus Vivit*, namely "inviting young people to events or occasions that provide an opportunity not only for learning, but also for conversing, celebrating, singing, listening to real stories and experiencing a shared encounter with the living God."[410]

The importance of connecting catechesis to the *kerygma* and to practical application in daily life are discussed in subsequent paragraphs in this section, as are the benefits of making young adults agent of their own formation.[411]

## CATECHESIS WITH ADULTS (paragraphs 257-265)

A particular concern for catechetical leaders has been how to realise the vision of the 1997 *General Directory for Catechesis* that formation in the faith is "a process of continuing conversion, which lasts for the whole of life."[412] In many places, catechesis is viewed, practically speaking, as a process that is completed in childhood, or at Confirmation, whichever comes first. The present *Directory* offers specific guidance for working towards a fuller realisation of lifelong faith formation. This begins with an understanding of the complexity of the lives of adults in the modern world – a "lively dynamism that incorporates the factors of family, culture, society" as well as one's own identity formation in the midst of "moments of transition."[413] This situation, it is reasoned, requires a formation that draws from and points toward the diversity of life experience. Various approaches of adults toward living out the faith are discussed in this section:

- believing adults, who live out their faith and want to get to know it better;
- adults who, although they have been baptised, have not been adequately

---

[408] *DC* 250.
[409] *DC* 251.
[410] *DC* 252; cf. *ChV* 204.
[411] *DC* 253-255.
[412] *GDC* 56; cf. *RM* 46.
[413] *DC* 257.

formed or have not brought Christian initiation to completion, and can be referred to as quasi-catechumens;

- baptised adults who, although they do not live out their faith on a regular basis, nonetheless seek out contact with the ecclesial community at particular times in life;
- adults who come from other Christian confessions or from other religious experiences;
- adults who return to the Catholic faith after having had experiences in the new religious movements;
- unbaptised adults, who are candidates for the catechumenate properly so called.[414]

Continuing to mature in the faith is a personal process related to the general identity development of the adult, a process that sometimes intersects with significant life events, roles and responsibilities that highlight the needs for a more mature faith as well as accompaniment by the community. Therefore, adult faith formation is both a personal and communal process – one oriented towards making adults "capable of taking their own experience of faith in hand and desirous of continuing to journey onward and grow."[415] In the service of this goal, the *Directory* proposes four "tasks of catechesis with adults":[416]

- *to elicit faith*, fostering a new beginning of faith-filled experience and making the most of the human and spiritual resources that are never extinguished in the depths of every person, in view of a free and personal resumption of the initial motivation in terms of attraction, gusto, and determination;
- *to purify the faith* from partial, misguided, or erroneous religious representations, helping the participants above all to recognise the limitations of these and to decide to seek out more authentic distillations of faith in view of the journey towards the fullness of life to which the Gospel calls;
- *to nourish faith* thanks in part to an experience of meaningful ecclesial relationships, promoting the formation of mature Christian consciences capable of giving the reason for their hope and ready for a serene and intelligent dialogue with contemporary culture;
- *to assist the sharing and witness of faith*, preparing spaces of sharing and service in the Church and in the world as ways of realising the task of manifesting the kingdom of God.[417]

---

[414] *DC* 258.
[415] *DC* 260.
[416] *DC* 261.
[417] *DC* 261.

The *Directory* outlines several criteria for assuring that catechesis is meaningful and capable of reaching its goals.[418] These include the inclusion of the whole community; the proposal of "concrete and characteristic experiences of the life of faith" that correspond with the needs of the whole person; the inclusion of adults not as recipients of, but active participants in, their catechesis; attention to their individual states in life and how they might order their everyday lives according to Gospel principles; and finally, co-ordination of adult formation with the pastoral care of families and youth and other dimensions of the faith, including liturgy, service, and socio-cultural factors.[419]

Finally, this section outlines nine forms of adult catechesis:

- catechesis as a genuine initiation into the faith, or the accompaniment of candidates for Baptism and the sacraments of initiation through the catechumenal experience;

- catechesis as new initiation into the faith, or the accompaniment of those who, although they have been baptised, have not completed initiation or are not in fact evangelised;

- catechesis as rediscovery of the faith through "listening centres" or other approaches, or a presentation in the vein of evangelisation intended for those referred to as fallen away;

- catechesis of the proclamation of the faith in environments of life, of work, of recreation, or on the occasion of demonstrations of popular piety or of pilgrimage to shrines;

- catechesis with couples on the occasion of marriage or in the celebration of sacraments for their children, which often becomes a point of departure for further catechetical experiences;

- catechesis for the exploration of the faith on the basis of Sacred Scripture, a document of the Magisterium, or the lives of the saints and witnesses to the faith;

- liturgical catechesis, which is aimed at deliberate participation in community celebrations;

- catechesis on moral, cultural, or sociopolitical issues aimed at participation in the life of society, so that this may be active and inspired by the faith;

- catechesis in the area of the specific formation of pastoral workers, which constitutes a privileged opportunity for journeys of faith.[420]

---

[418] *DC* 262.
[419] *DC* 262.
[420] *DC* 264.

This list might be helpful to leaders who are planning a programme of adult catechesis so that they might reflect on the various contexts of adult formation and be mindful of creating an itinerary that presents a systematic overview of topics (and opportunities for active participation and application) as well as helping to meet the needs of adults who are at different points in their faith journeys. The *Directory* also points out the valuable contributions of various associations and movements to the formation of adults.[421]

## CATECHESIS WITH THE ELDERLY (paragraphs 266-268)

In his Apostolic Exhortation to young people, *Christus Vivit*, Pope Francis is critical of a type of superficial idealisation of youthfulness that devalues the elderly.[422] He points out that Scripture "encourages us to remain close to the elderly, so that we can benefit from their experience."[423] The *Directory for Catechesis* begins the section on catechesis with the elderly with the same sentiment, calling older adults "a patrimony of memory, and often keepers of the values of a society" and highlighting the importance of their pastoral care.[424]

The twentieth century developmental psychologist Erik Erikson referred to the later years as a time in which an individual reflects on the totality of one's life and its meaning, either feeling a sense of integrity, purpose, and success in how one has lived one's life, or a sense of despair and dread. The Catholic faith can be a tremendous support, an organising principle as elderly adults navigate this stage of life and seek answers to existential questions. The *Directory* presents several different ways that an examination of the faith can be profoundly helpful to individuals in later years, including offering the hope of meeting God after death, providing enlightenment, and facilitating healing.[425] The gifts of experience and wisdom that elderly persons possess, the *Directory* notes, also make many older persons natural catechists for the community.[426]

## CATECHESIS WITH PERSONS WITH DISABILITIES (paragraphs 269-272)

The *Directory* calls the catechetical community to be open and welcoming towards persons with disabilities, reminding us that they have a "call to faith that is good and full of meaning."[427] Quoting a message Pope Francis gave to a convention for persons with disabilities, the *Directory* points out that as is true of each individual, persons with disabilities bring not only needs, but also gifts to share with the Christian community.

---

[421] *DC* 264.
[422] *ChV* 183.
[423] *DC* 188.
[424] *DC* 266.
[425] *DC* 267.
[426] *DC* 268.
[427] *DC* 269.

We are admonished, therefore to pay attention both to "the possibility to educate in the faith the people with even grave or very grave disabilities" and to be willing "to consider them as active subjects in the community in which they live."[428] This perspective towards persons with disabilities is presented as a contrast to that found in the larger society, which often takes a utilitarian view towards human life, rather than seeing the inherent dignity of all persons. In addition, the *Directory* notes, the presence and active participation of persons with disabilities can be a "growth opportunity for the ecclesial community," as this can prompt the large Christian community to "overcome cultural prejudice."[429] the presence of persons with disabilities can cause discomfort and even fear, the *Directory* acknowledges, because they are reminders of the fragility inherent to the human condition, a fragility that includes both suffering and eventual death for every human person. However, this is an important gift of persons with disabilities. They are "witnesses to the essential truths of human life," and they help us to "interpret the mystery of human suffering in the light of the death and resurrection of Jesus Christ."[430]

The *Directory* calls us to be open to the presence of persons with disabilities and to seek out "new channels of communication and methods more suitable for fostering the encounter with Jesus Christ."[431] This will include the use of methods that involve

---

[428] *DC* 270; cf. Francis, *Address to Participants in the Convention for Persons with Disabilities* (11th June 2016).
[429] *DC* 270.
[430] *DC* 270.
[431] *DC* 271.

multiple senses and various ways of receiving information and responding – including auditory, visual and kinaesthetic formats. This section points out that catechists will also likely need particular formation for catechesis with persons with disabilities.

"No one can refuse the sacraments to persons with disabilities," the *Directory* boldly proclaims, stating that these persons, like all others, are "called to the fullness of sacramental life."[432] Furthermore, individuals with disabilities should be involved, the *Directory* asserts, not only as recipients of catechesis, but as participants and leaders.

### CATECHESIS WITH MIGRANTS (paragraphs 273-276)

Migration occurs for a number of different reasons, the *Directory* points out, including dramatic and challenging circumstances such as poverty, armed conflict, climate change, persecution and violence as well as more mundane situations such as urbanisation and the availability of better positions and salaries in other locations. In one way or another, "all of the particular Churches are involved" in migration – either as locations of origin, transit, or destination.[433] The process of migration can lead to serious issues, such as "grave humanitarian problems...abandonment of religious practice, and a crisis for the convictions of faith."[434]

Quoting an address on migration by Pope Francis, the *Directory* reminds us that the Church is "a mother without boundaries and without borders."[435] The Church's catechetical responsibilities related to migration include offering spiritual support to migrants in order to facilitate their continued trust in God as well as educating the larger Christian community regarding their "duty of solidarity" and addressing prejudice and discrimination towards migrants that occurs in the larger society and can even occur within the Church.[436] The community should also be educated regarding the cultural traditions of migrants and make efforts to provide programming in their language, so as not to add to "the many disruptions they have already experienced."[437] Migrants can also "become proclaimers of the Gospel" in their new communities, thus "enriching the spiritual fabric" of the community.[438] Dialogue and collaboration between the Church of origin and the Church of reception can help in providing catechesis in the language and tradition of migrants and helps to form catechists who are competent to minister to migrant communities.[439]

---

[432] *DC* 272.

[433] *DC* 273.

[434] *DC* 273.

[435] *DC* 274; cf. Francis, *Address to Participants in the Seventh Congress for the Pastoral Care of Migrants* (21st November 2014).

[436] *DC,* 274.

[437] *DC* 275.

[438] *DC* 275.

[439] *DC* 276.

### CATECHESIS WITH EMIGRANTS (paragraphs 277-278)

The section on catechesis of emigrants covers two topics – assistance in the countries of emigration and catechesis in the countries of origin. On the first subject, the *Directory* points out that the completion of the process of migration and the stabilisation in the new place does not end the relationship between Churches of origin and those who have travelled elsewhere, as continued collaboration can assist in setting up chaplaincies, missions, and other services that will assist emigrants in their new homes.[440] These ministries often include catechetical functions, such as programmes for Christian initiation and ongoing formation in faith. the *Directory* points out that this work, like all catechesis, should be conducted in co-operation with the local bishop.[441]

With regard to catechesis in countries of origin, the *Directory* mentions that emigrants often return to their countries of origin for brief periods of time for various reasons, including traditional local celebrations. It is recommended here that these events have catechetical dimensions and when emigrants request to celebrate sacraments in their countries of origin, priests ensure that there has been adequate preparation as well as the appropriate co-ordination with pastors in the country of emigration.[442]

### CATECHESIS WITH MARGINAL PERSONS (paragraphs 279-282)

The *Directory* defines *marginal persons* as "those who are close or have already fallen into marginalisation," including those in situations of poverty, exploitation, homelessness, chronic illness, and other challenging circumstances.[443] The preferential option for the poor that is demonstrated by Jesus Christ in the Gospels and is a foundation of Catholic social teaching is continued in the solidarity and outreach shown by Christian communities towards marginal persons. The *Directory* reminds us that the people of God "must always be vigilant and ready to identify new works of mercy and to practise them with generosity and enthusiasm."[444]

Quoting Pope Francis's Apostolic Exhortation, *Evangelii Gaudium*, the *Directory* reiterates that the lack of spiritual care is the "worst discrimination which the poor suffer,"[445] often due to the lack of access to pastoral resources because of systemic issues. This underscores the need for the Christian community to be ready to respond in ways that are often less traditional: "in informal contexts and environments and with casual methods" in order to provide both an initial encounter with the *kerygma*

---

[440] *DC* 277.
[441] *DC* 277.
[442] *DC* 278.
[443] *DC* 279.
[444] *DC* 279.
[445] *DC* 280; cf. *EG* 200.

and ongoing formation in a way that meets the diverse needs of those who are marginalised.[446]

The final paragraphs of this section are devoted to a discussion of catechesis in prison, which the *Directory* describes as "authentic mission territory" and a "frontier laboratory for pastoral action."[447] God can speak in any environment, including in prison, where incarcerated persons can have an opportunity to experience the true freedom that is found in Jesus Christ. The *Directory* highlights the importance of proclaiming the *kerygma* in prison settings, focusing in particular on the Gospel themes of forgiveness and liberation and allowing prisoners to experience a "direct encounter with Sacred Scripture."[448] Those who are involved in catechesis in prisons make "God's presence visible in the signs of unconditional acceptance and attentive listening," and show to prisoners the "motherly face of the Church."[449] The chapter concludes with a reminder to also accompany family members of prisoners and those who have completed their terms of incarceration, who face a number of obstacles and challenges as they work towards reintegrating in the larger society.[450]

## QUESTIONS FOR REFLECTION

1 With what age(s) do you work in catechesis?
   • How can knowledge gleaned from the human sciences assist you in meeting the unique learning needs of this population?
2 Who is at the peripheries in the community you serve?
   • How might you help to welcome and include those who are marginalised?

---

[446] *DC* 280.
[447] *DC* 281.
[448] *DC* 282.
[449] *DC* 282.
[450] *DC* 282.

# A Prayer for Catechists

GOD OF ALL AGES,
You revealed yourself progressively to humanity
as we were able to hear and understand.
Send your Holy Spirit now to inspire us
with the wisdom to meet each learner
at his or her level of understanding.
Help us also as we work to engage and support
    the family, the domestic Church,
and help us to include all persons in our work,
especially those with disabilities
and others who are sometimes marginalised.
We ask this in the name of Christ Jesus.
Amen.

## CHAPTER IX:

# The Christian Community as Participant in Catechesis

### THE CHURCH AND THE MINISTRY OF GOD'S WORD (paragraphs 283-289)

Part Three of the *Directory* for Catechesis, titled, "Catechesis in the Particular Churches", begins with a chapter on the role of the community in catechesis. Central to the role of the community in forming faith is the centrality of the Word of God in the mission of the Church. "The ministry of the Word", the *Directory* states, "is born from listening and educated believers in the art of listening, because only those who listen can proclaim."[451] As Pope Francis states in *Evangelii Gaudium*, "All evangelisation is based on that Word. Listened to, meditated upon, lived, celebrated, and witnessed to. The Sacred Scriptures are the very source of evangelisation."[452] The *Directory* describes a Church that has an attitude of *docibilitas* toward the Word of God, placing herself at the service of God's word, which is "the origin of the Church's very mission."[453]

The task of the Church with regard to Sacred Scripture is one of mediation, according to the *Directory* – proclaiming it, transmitting it faithfully through the

---

[451] *DC* 283.
[452] *EG* 174; cf. *DC* 283.
[453] *DC* 284.

generations, and interpreting it through the Magisterium.[454] The *Directory* speaks of the close relationship between the ministry of the Word and the ministry of the sacraments, arguing, as Pope Benedict did, that it is impossible fully to understand one without the other.[455]

If the Word of God is the origin of evangelisation, the people of God are its agent.[456] Anointed by the Holy Spirit, the Church participates in Christ's mission as prophet, drawing upon the *sensus fidei*, through which she is able "to discern, bear witness to, and proclaim the word of God."[457] Catechesis, which is inextricably intertwined with evangelisation, is also a responsibility of the entire community, since all the baptised are missionary disciples; however, we are all called to different roles in this task through the diverse gifts we receive.[458]

Encounter, accompaniment, and dialogue are skills that are essential to evangelisation in modern times, and these skills are modelled, learned, and utilised in *synodal practice*, which gathers the faithful of different ages, positions, and perspectives in order to discern God's call for the Church in particular contexts and situations. The *Directory* identifies three ways that synodal practice "proposes important goals for evangelisation: it brings about the joint discernment of what paths should be taken; leads to acting in synergy with everyone's gifts; and protects against the isolation of opposing sides or of individuals."[459] In a time in which our world, and even our Church, has become increasingly ideologically polarised, the art of dialogue and its fruit of mutual understanding are especially important, not only as essential tools for evangelisation, but also as a witness of Christian charity. Let us not forget the early Christians, whom Scripture describes as being "of one heart and mind",[460] prompting the pagans of Tertullian's time to remark, "Look how they love one another."[461]

## THE EASTERN CHURCHES (paragraphs 290-292)

The next section of the *Directory* is devoted to the Eastern Churches, describing their liturgies and traditions as "treasures" that "have always contributed to evangelisation."[462] The role of catechesis in helping the Eastern Churches preserve their traditions and identity is emphasised here. Quoting from a document from the

---

[454] *DC* 285.
[455] *DC* 286; cf. Benedict XVI, *Verbum Domini* (30th September 2010), 55.
[456] *DC* 287.
[457] *DC* 287.
[458] *DC* 287-288; cf. *EG* 120.
[459] *DC* 289.
[460] *Acts* 4:32 (NABRE).
[461] *Apologeticus* ch. 39, sect. 7.
[462] *DC* 290.

Congregation for the Oriental Churches, the *Directory* highlights the strong connection between catechesis and liturgy in the Eastern Churches, and how this is connected in a meaningful way with the catechesis of the early Church, which revealed the faith to catechumens and new initiates through immersion in the liturgical rites of the Church.[463] Clergy and catechists are encouraged to be familiar with the rite and norms related to Eastern Churches, especially those working in areas where *sui iuris* Churches (autonomous Eastern Churches in communion with the Roman Catholic Church) are present.[464]

## THE PARTICULAR CHURCHES (paragraphs 293-297)

The next section of the *Directory* refers to the dioceses, archdioceses, and their equivalents, called *particular Churches* because they contain all of the "essential structures of the Church: "the Gospel, the sacraments, the episcopate, which with the assistance of the priests presides over pastoral care."[465] While the particular Church is "fully Church", the *Directory* asserts, "she is not so on her own, but in the communion of all the Churches."[466] The particular Church is a source of evangelisation because it is the vehicle through which people "enter into contact with a community."[467] The *Directory* calls particular Churches to be open to "bringing the word of God to the farthest reaches, opening oneself to all types of peripheries."[468] Particular Churches also evangelise, the *Directory* states, "by rooting themselves in the history, the culture, the traditions, the languages, and the problems of their people."[469]

As function of the mission to evangelise, everyone within a particular Church is responsible for catechesis – in particular the local bishop and those commissioned by him, who are called to act according to the norms of the Church and as her agents in co-operation with the bishop.[470] The *Directory* calls particular Churches to catechetical renewal, given the current circumstances that exist in many dioceses around the world; in particular, the "pressing need to frame everything in terms of evangelisation" and the need to reach people who are not connecting with our traditional contexts and forms of catechesis.[471]

---

[463] *DC* 291; cf. Congregation for the Oriental Churches, *Instruction for the Application of the Liturgical Prescriptions of the Code of Canons of the Eastern Church* (6th January 1996), 10.
[464] *DC* 292.
[465] *DC* 293.
[466] *DC* 293.
[467] *DC* 294.
[468] *DC* 295.
[469] *DC* 295.
[470] *DC* 296.
[471] *DC* 297.

## PARISHES (paragraphs 298-303)

Parishes are individual cells of the particular Church and the most visible communities of Christians for people in the area where they are located.[472] The *Directory* describes three pillars on which parishes are founded: the word of God, sacraments and charity.[473] Echoing the Congregation for the Clergy's recent admonition that parishes should "go out of themselves, offering instruments for reform, even structural, in a spirit of communion and collaboration, of encounter and closeness, of mercy and solicitude for the proclamation of the Gospel,"[474] the *Directory* states that parishes should press "forward in the direction of evangelisation," and emphasises the importance of "self-renewal" and "constant adaptivity" in this task.[475] Echoing the words of Pope St John Paul II, the *Directory* envisions the parish as a "community of communities" in which movements and small groups are included and supported.[476]

The *Directory* calls parishes to view catechesis through the lens of missionary conversion, taking into account the new cultural and social contexts in which their members live.[477] The present *Directory* reaffirms the *GDC*'s view of the parish as "the privileged place of education in the faith," but cautions us to remain aware that the parish "is not the centre of gravity for all catechetical functions."[478] We are challenged to "rethink in a missionary vein all the pastoral activities of the Christian community, even the most ordinary and traditional ones."[479] To this end, and for the renewal of catechesis specifically, the *Directory* proposes several aspects for consideration:[480]

- *"Community of missionary disciples"*, where people live out their faith.

- *"Missionary mentality"* in which one moves from preconceived notions to an openness toward the Holy Spirit, prompting catechesis "to decentralise and to set itself to listen and go forth toward the life experiences of people, illuminating them with the light of the Gospel."[481]

- *"Formative offerings inspired by the catechumenate"*: catechetical offerings that familiarise persons of all ages with the *kerygma* and are connected to other pastoral activities.

---

[472] *DC* 298.
[473] *DC* 299.
[474] Congregation for the Clergy, *Instruction "The pastoral conversion of the Parish community in the service of the evangelising mission of the Church"*, 20th July 2020.
[475] *DC* 300.
[476] *DC* 301; cf. St John Paul II, *Ecclesia in America* (22nd January 1999): 41.
[477] *DC* 302.
[478] *DC* cf. *GDC* 257.
[479] *DC* 303.
[480] *DC* 303.
[481] *DC* 303.

## ASSOCIATIONS, MOVEMENTS, AND GROUPS OF THE FAITHFUL
(paragraphs 304-308)

The next section of the *Directory* concentrates on associations, movements, and other groups and their role in evangelisation and catechesis. Common elements of these groups are discussed, including "the rediscovery of the community dimension; the reinforcement of aspects of Christian life like listening to the Word, the practice of piety, [and] charity; [and] the promotion of the laity in the mission of Church and society."[482]

The relationship between associations and movements and the parishes and dioceses where they operate can be a complex one. On the parish level, especially, the more serious challenges can include territorial disputes, elitism, and an insular tendency that sometimes sees various groups concentrating within and failing to connect in meaningful ways with the larger parish or community. Still, as the *Directory* reiterates, the Church has long recognised the right of the faithful to association,[483] and associations and movements can enrich the Church and give individuals a place to explore their interests and use their gifts. The *Directory* asserts that the keys to capitalising on the gifts of associations and movements while overcoming the challenges can be found in the criteria of ecclesiality articulated by St John Paul II – namely, "the primacy given to each Christian's call to holiness; the responsibility of professing the Catholic faith; the witness to a strong and authentic communion in filial relationship to the pope and the bishop; conformity to and participation in the Church's apostolic goal; [and] a commitment to a presence in human society."[484] As examples, the *Directory* points to basic ecclesial communities, common in Latin America, which are typically groups within a particular neighbourhood that meet together, study Scripture, and reflect on its relevance to their current situations.[485]

The *Directory* is careful to point out that the formation that occurs in movements and associations, while important, tends to concentrate on the particular charism of the group, and should not be considered a replacement for more systematic and comprehensive catechesis, and time should be set aside for the latter as well.[486] Where more comprehensive catechesis occurs within the context of these groups, the following aspects are given for consideration:[487]

---

[482] *DC* 304.

[483] *DC* 305.

[484] *DC* (nn. 26); cf. St John Paul II, *Christifideles Laici* (30th December 1988): 30.

[485] *DC* 306.

[486] *DC* 307.

[487] *DC* 308.

- catechesis is invariably a work of the Church, and therefore the principle of the ecclesiality of catechesis always needs to be evident. The particular associations, movements, and groups will therefore attune themselves to the diocesan pastoral plans;

- it is necessary to respect the distinctive nature of catechesis, developing all its richness and forming participants in all the dimensions of the Christian life, according to the sensibility and the style of apostolate unique to each charism;

- the parish is called to appreciate the catechesis that takes place in the aggregations because this often engages people more comprehensively and reaches beyond the parish boundaries.

## CATHOLIC SCHOOLS (paragraphs 309-312)

Evangelisation is a primary function of Catholic schools. Catholic schools are agents of the Church, *"ecclesial subjects"*, that make "the Church's mission visible above all in the fields of education and culture."[488] Catholic schools should, and must, be more than non-denominational schools that also happen to have religion classes. Speaking about the role of the Catholic school, the Vatican II Declaration on Christian Education, *Gravissimum Educationis* states, "But its proper function is to create for the school community a special atmosphere animated by the Gospel spirit of freedom and charity, to help youth grow according to the new creatures they were made through

---

[488] *DC* 311.

Baptism as they develop their own personalities, and finally to order the whole of human culture to the news of salvation so that the knowledge the students gradually acquire of the world, life and man is illumined by faith".[489] A key role of the Catholic school, then, is as an agent of evangelisation. The Catholic school accomplishes this through several characteristics, which are articulated in the *Directory for Catechesis*: "harmony with the formative aims of secular schools; an educational community permeated by evangelical values; attention to young people; [and]concern for teaching the integration of faith, culture, and life."[490]

Quoting the Congregation for Catholic Education, the *Directory* highlights the transition from viewing Catholic schools as institutions to understanding that they are communities. The *Directory* adds that they are *communities of faith* "that have at their foundation an educational initiative characterised by evangelical values."[491] Success in this mission, the *Directory* asserts, requires "the involvement of the whole school community, parents as well, always placing students at the centre."[492]

## THE TEACHING OF THE CATHOLIC RELIGION IN SCHOOLS (paragraphs 313-318)

At the end of the previous section, the *Directory* acknowledges that parents choose Catholic schools for a variety of reasons (and schools should respect this in their interaction with parents), but affirms that catechesis and religious education should be coherent, comprehensive, and presented in connection with the rest of the formation offered by the school in the interest of forming the whole person.[493] Quoting from a document from the Congregation for Catholic Education, the *Directory* draws a distinction between catechesis and religious education: "Catechesis promotes personal adherence to Christ and the maturing of the Christian life, [whilst] school teaching gives the students knowledge about Christianity's identity and the Christian life."[494] Catechesis and education about the Catholic religion, therefore, are complementary, but not the same. Even in contexts of religious pluralism (e.g., in some communities where only a minority of Catholic school students are Catholic), teaching the Catholic religion and connecting it to other academic disciplines are important to forming the whole person,[495] and it can sometimes be the only exposure students have to the Gospel message.[496]

---

[489] *GE* 8.

[490] *DC* 309.

[491] *DC* 310; cf. Congregation for Catholic Education, *The Catholic School on the Threshold of the Third Millennium* (28th December 1997): 11.

[492] *DC* 310.

[493] *DC* 312.

[494] *DC* 313; cf. Congregation for Catholic Education, *Educating to Intercultural Dialogue in Catholic Schools: Living in Harmony for a Civilisation of Love* (28th October 2013), 74.

[495] *DC* 314.

[496] *DC* 313.

Religious education in Catholic schools should be just as rigorous, the *Directory* asserts, as other academic areas, but should also include open dialogue, particularly in contexts where conflicts about faith extend into the larger society.[497] Dialogue is also important given the number of families where members of different Christian denominations are present. [498]

While there is no one model of religious education that is appropriate to all Catholic schools, the *Directory* instructs episcopal conferences to ensure that textbooks are available for use in Catholic school religious education.[499] The fruitfulness of the teaching of religion in Catholic schools, according to the *Directory*, depends on the ability of the teacher to connect "faith and culture, human and religious components, science and religion, school and other educational agencies."[500] Finally, the *Directory* states that while the task of the teacher in the teaching of the Catholic religion in Catholic schools is purely educational, teachers should "be believers committed to personal growth in the faith, incorporated into a Christian community, desirous of giving the reason for their faith through their professional expertise as well."[501]

## QUESTIONS FOR REFLECTION

1   Of the three aspects proposed in this chapter for the renewal of catechesis in the parish (community of missionary disciples, missionary mentality, and formative offerings inspired by the catechumenate), which aspect would benefit from particular attention at your parish?
    • How might you contribute to an increased focus in this area?

2   What associations and movements exists in your diocese and parish?
    • How might these groups contribute to catechesis?

---

[497] *DC* 315.
[498] *DC* 317.
[499] *DC* 316.
[500] *DC* 318.
[501] *DC* 318.

# A Prayer for Catechists

Ever-loving Lord,
You have created us for relationship and communion
with you and one another.
Help us, as a community of believers,
to be unified in our catechetical mission.
May we use our diverse gifts and love
for one another as a witness of your truth.
We ask this in the name of Christ Jesus.
Amen.

CHAPTER X:

# Catechesis in the Face of Contemporary Scenarios

C hapter ten of the *Directory* begins by explaining that, because catechesis takes place in a Church that exists within the human community, it naturally has both cultural and social dimensions.[502] Indeed it must if it is to be connected in any way with daily life. And because catechesis exists within a society and culture, if must also be "a prophetic sign of promotion of the fullness of life for all," including "opposing processes focused on injustice, on the exclusion of the poor, on the primacy of money."[503]

## CATECHESIS IN SITUATIONS OF PLURALISM AND COMPLEXITY
(paragraphs 320-342)

The *Directory* points out how globalisation and communications media have led to increased connections and interdependence, and this has led to increased complexity in contemporary culture, including a plurality of religious and political viewpoints.[504] In his Apostolic Exhortation, *Evangelii Gaudium*, Pope Francis likened the nature of today's complex cultural reality to a *polyhedron*, a three dimensional figure with multiple distinct sides that help form the whole.[505]

---

[502] *DC* 319.
[503] *DC* 319.
[504] *DC* 320.
[505] *DC* 231; cf. *EG* 236.

This complex reality, and the resulting presence of multiple viewpoints in contemporary society, calls, the *Directory* asserts, for a *synodal* model of evangelisation in which the community journeys together, each bringing their diverse viewpoints and actively participating.[506] In terms of religious pluralism specifically, however, the *Directory* warns against the indifference, insensitivity, or relativism that can develop among Christians when they are living in a multi-religious environment.[507] We must have respect for, and sensitivity to, the different religious worldviews in our community while also fostering a strong sense of Catholic identity. In fact, the *Directory* asserts, the value placed on the freedom to choose one's religious viewpoint (or none at all) is an opportunity to encourage a well-reasoned and mature personal faith, and this once again points to the essential connection between catechesis and evangelisation.[508]

The socio-cultural reality of increased globalisation (in part due to mass communication) comes with both blessings and challenges, the *Directory* states.[509] On the one hand, we might have a stronger sense of a global community in which we are called to be engaged and are all responsible to one another. On the other hand, such globalisation can encourage conformity and uniformity. In addition, the explosion of information technology has given equal footing to many different voices and messages, and this results in the need to foster skills in critical thinking and discernment.

The *Directory* again appeals to us to make use of research in the human sciences, this time in service of uncovering the "foundation of cultures"[510] and engaging in dialogue in the "*junctures of existence, anthropological environments,* and *modern areopagi,*"[511] the latter being a reference to the Areopagus, or public square, which was the city centre of dialogue in ancient Greek culture. In other words, we are called here to engage in dialogue with key thinkers, artists, and leaders in our society in the spaces where they gather, in an effort to shape society and illuminate the conversation with Gospel values, which speak to the deepest needs of every human being.[512]

In the paragraphs that follow, this dialogue with culture is discussed in four different contexts: urban, rural, traditional local cultures, and popular piety. Regarding the urban context, the *Directory* points out that in cities today, cultural models are no longer generated by the Christian community, and indeed sometimes contrast with the Christian worldview; however, the religious sense is still present in the life

---

[506] *DC* 321.

[507] *DC* 322.

[508] *DC* 322.

[509] *DC* 323.

[510] *DC* 324; cf. Francis, *Address to Participants at the International Pastoral Congress on the World's Big Cities* (27th November 2014).

[511] *DC* 324.

[512] *DC* 325.

of the city, and the Church is called to observe and reflect on how God is present there.[513] As Christians, we can proclaim the *kerygma*, the saving message of Jesus Christ, as a message of hope that speaks in sharp contrast to the despair, inequity, poverty and violence that has taken root in so many of our cities.[514] A catechesis inspired by the accompaniment of the community we find in the catechumenate also presents a hopeful antidote to the isolation experienced by so many individuals in urban contexts.[515]

Increasing urbanisation has challenged rural communities to maintain their identities, both sociologically and physically.[516] The *Directory* reminds us of the catechetical importance of the rural environment, both as a locus of care for God's creation and the simplicity and freedom from consumerism that can often be found in the countryside.[517] In addition, rural contexts provide us vivid practical illustrations of biblical metaphors and parables, with their many references to sowing and reaping, caring for flocks, etc.

Traditional cultures have been adversely affected, the *Directory* notes, by the pressure for conformity, the ubiquitous communications media, and migration that are by-products of globalisation, sometimes to the extent of loss of culture traditions and identity.[518] The *Directory* reiterates the need to respect the diverse traditions found in traditional cultures and to look for the seeds of faith that can be found there.[519] Catechesis with indigenous peoples involves "getting to know" the people, examining the culture "in the light of the Gospel" and manifesting "the fullness and newness of the Lord Jesus."[520] This requires an openness on the part of the catechist and an understanding that the same truths of the Gospel might be expressed in different ways through diverse culture lenses.[521] The following directives are offered for catechists who work with indigenous peoples:[522] "Catechists who work among indigenous peoples are to take care":

- not to go in their own name and alone, but sent by the local Church and, even better, in a group with other missionary disciples;
- to present themselves as successors of the previous work of evangelisation, if there has been any;

---

[513] *DC* 326.
[514] *DC* 327.
[515] *DC* 328.
[516] *DC* 329.
[517] *DC* 330.
[518] *DC* 331.
[519] *DC* 332.
[520] *DC* 333.
[521] *DC* 334.
[522] *DC* 335.

- to show immediately that they are motivated only by the faith and not by political or economic intentions, expressing closeness above all with the infirm, the poorest, and children;

- to strive to get to know the indigenous language, ceremonies, customs, always showing great respect;

- to participate in the ceremonies and celebrations, knowing how to intervene at the appropriate time to suggest a few modifications, if necessary, especially if there is a danger of religious syncretism;

- to organise catechesis by age groups and celebrate the sacraments, making good use of the traditional celebrations.

The *Directory* describes popular piety as both evidence of inculturation of the faith and opportunity for catechesis. Popular devotions, and particularly cultural-specific forms of popular piety, often develop as a result of the intersection between cultural traditions and the proclamation of the faith in a specific cultural context. Popular piety is a "valuable treasure"[523] with "undeniable spiritual significance"[524] because it reflects and responds to the thirst for God in every culture, and particularly among persons living in poverty. It is also a sign of hope.

Still, popular piety is vulnerable to superstitions and theological misunderstandings, so it is important to provide guidance to communities who are practising popular devotions.[525] The *Directory* points out the "evangelising power" of popular piety.[526] Indeed, in catechesis we can use popular devotions as a familiar starting point from which to unpack the mysteries of the faith and draw connections to the practice of the faith as well. Pilgrimage to shrines is discussed in this section of the *Directory* as a particular manifestation of popular piety that speaks to the need to get away from daily life and provides an opportunity to rediscover the power of the Gospel message.[527]

## CATECHESIS IN THE CONTEXT OF ECUMENISM AND RELIGIOUS PLURALISM

As the *Directory* points out, increased mobility has led to more and more encounter between peoples with different religious views.[528] Pope Benedict pointed to division between Christians as an obstacle to leading others to Christ.[529] Like his predecessors, Pope Francis has encouraged increased dialogue between Catholics and non-Catholic

---

[523] *DC* 336.
[524] *DC* 337.
[525] *DC* 339.
[526] *DC* 340.
[527] *DC* 341-342.
[528] *DC* 343.
[529] Benedict XVI, *Address at Ecumenical Prayer Service*, St Joseph's Parish, New York (18th April 2008).

Christians, and between Catholics and members of other religions. Such dialogue has multiple implications for catechesis. With regard to ecumenism, we must not tire of working towards the unity of all Christians, because a more unified Church is a clearer witness of the truth of Jesus Christ. In our encounters with individuals of other Christian Churches or confessions, we can use as a starting point our common belief in a Trinitarian God, in Scripture, the Sacrament of Baptism, and, the *Directory* notes, martyrdom, which is not just our historical heritage, but a reality of the situation Christians today face in many places around the world.[530] Regarding catechesis in contexts of divisions among Christians, the *Directory* directs us to "take care":

- to affirm that division is a grave wound that contradicts the Lord's will, and that Catholics are called upon to participate actively in the ecumenical movement, above all with prayer;

- to expound clearly and with charity the doctrine of the Catholic faith 'respecting in a particular way the order of the hierarchy of truths and avoiding expressions and ways of presenting doctrine which would be an obstacle to dialogue';

---

[530] *DC* 344; cf. Francis, *Homily at vespers on the Solemnity of the Conversion of St Paul the Apostle* (25th January 2016).

- to present in a correct manner the teaching of the other Churches and ecclesial communities, showing what unites Christians and explaining, including with brief historical citations, what divides.[531]

As catechists, we are called to foster a desire for unity and a respect for the beliefs of other Christians, even as we take care to preserve our Catholic identity.[532] The *Directory* calls us to collaborate, where possible, in catechetical efforts with non-Catholic Christians, even if that collaboration is necessarily limited in some ways by our differences.[533]

Both St John Paul II and Benedict XVI met with and prayed with other Christians, and dialogued with adherents of other faiths – especially our Jewish and Muslim neighbours, who share our belief in the God of Abraham. Regarding the Jewish faith, the *Directory* cautions against presenting Judaism as "simply another religion, because Christianity has Jewish roots and the relationships between the two traditions are unique."[534] In addition, as Catholics we believe that Scripture presents a coherent and progressive history of salvation in which the Jewish faith plays a decisive role. Indeed, the covenants of God with the Jewish people were not replaced by Christ, but rather fulfilled in him.

With regard to other religious faiths, and especially in contexts of religious pluralism, the *Directory* directs us to reflect on the truths that we hold in common and to be attentive in our catechesis to "deepening and strengthening the *identity* of believers," helping Catholics "grow in discernment with respect to the other religions," and encouraging "a missionary impulse of witness to the faith; of collaboration in defense of human dignity; of affable and cordial dialogue, and where possible, of the explicit proclamation of the Gospel."[535] We are advised to take special care in our relationship with Muslims, fostering "understanding and encounter" as a means of promoting peace and healthy relationships with our Muslim neighbours.

The *Directory* closes the section on catechesis in contexts of religious pluralism with several paragraphs about new religious movements, especially those that appropriate some symbolism or language of Christianity but also deviate from it in significant ways. As the *Directory* suggests, these movements can be attractive to individuals who were raised in Christian environments but for whatever reason did not find fulfilment or reach a mature faith.[536] In the context of new religious movements, we are called to emphasise the proclamation of the *kerygma*, "striving to make the Church a true community," promoting knowledge of Scripture and authentic doctrine,

---

[531] *DC* 345.
[532] *DC* 345.
[533] *DC* 346.
[534] *DC* 348.
[535] *DC* 350.
[536] *DC* 352.

and "paying attention to the symbols, gestures, and ceremonies of the liturgy and of popular piety, not downplaying the affective dimension that more easily touches the human heart."[537]

## CATECHESIS IN SOCIO-CULTURAL CONTEXTS

### Catechesis and the Scientific Mentality (paragraphs 354-358)

Since the time of the Enlightenment, there have been those who would pit science and faith against one another. This is a false dichotomy. Albert Einstein famously said, "A legitimate conflict between science and religion cannot exist. Science without religion is lame, religion without science is blind."[538] In a 1988 letter to Fr George V. Coyne, then Director of the Vatican Observatory, St John Paul II wrote, "Science can purify religion from error and superstition; religion can purify science from idolatry and false absolutes. Each can draw the other into a wider world, a world in which both can flourish... We need each other to be what we must be, what we are called to be."[539]

As a result of being formed in a secular society that often seeks to compartmentalise faith from other aspects of life, many individuals, especially young people, feel a disconnect between the faith and science. However, the Catholic Church has little disagreement with modern science.[540] Historically speaking, the Church has been a patron of the sciences. For example, Georges Lemaitre, the physicist who developed the Big Bang theory, was a Catholic priest. Gregor Mendel, the father of genetics, was an Augustinian friar.

One source of confusion is the idea that one must choose between faith and science as a source of truth. On the contrary, there are truths we know by faith and facts we glean from science. The Catholic Church does not teach that the first chapter of *Genesis* is meant to teach science. The Catholic Church has never denounced the theory of evolution as opposed to faith, because *Genesis* teaches the theological truth that God created the world, but does not attempt to explain, in a scientific manner, the process he used to do so. In 1950, Pope Pius XII proclaimed there was no intrinsic opposition between evolution and Catholic doctrine.[541] In 1996, St John Paul II endorsed Pius's statement.[542]

---

[537] *DC* 353.

[538] Einstein, A., "About Religion", *Ideas and Opinions*, Seelig C. (ed.) (New York, Modern Library, 1994) p.49.

[539] St John Paul II, *Letter to Reverend George V. Coyne, S.J., Director of the Vatican Observatory* (1st June 1988).

[540] Cf. *CCC* 159.

[541] Pius XII, *Humani Generis* (1950): 36.

[542] St John Paul II, *Message to the Pontifical Academy of Sciences: On Evolution* (22nd October 1996).

The *Directory* stresses the need for catechists to promote a correct understanding of the relationship between science and faith,[543] to help those to whom we minister avoid falling into the fallacies of reductionism or scientism (reducing all human phenomena to their physical properties alone).[544] We are also called to promote the use of advances in science and technology to protect and improve human life and to promote the common good.[545]

The *Directory* advises catechists to be aware of the preconceived notions about science and faith that their participants might carry with them into the catechetical process, to avoid oversimplifications regarding these issues, to utilise "the witness of Christian scientists", and to be familiar with "the main documents of the Magisterium that deal with the relationship between faith and reason, between theology and science."[546] We are also called to evangelise and offer pastoral support to women and men of science and to foster an inculturation of the faith in the scientific world.[547]

## Catechesis and Digital Culture (paragraphs 359-372)

The *Directory* devotes several paragraphs to the realm of digital technology, which it describes as a distinct culture,[548] with *digital natives* (those who have grown up immersed in the digital world) and *digital immigrants* (people who came of age before technological advances like widespread use of the Internet and various digital platforms and devices). The *Directory* reflects upon the profound influence the digital world has on ideas, our understanding of ourselves and the world, and our values.[549] The Internet and digital media are highlighted as forums for reaching and involving young people in pastoral initiatives and activities,[550] but the *Directory* also warns about the risk of addiction, isolation and gradual loss of contact with concrete reality.[551] The latter is a particular risk for Catholics, since the physical gathering of the faithful in community and the involvement of all five senses in the sacraments are so integral to our faith.

The *Directory* calls catechists to proclaim the Gospel in the "language of the new generations" and to invite them "to create a new sense of community" that includes, but "is not exhausted by, what they find online."[552] Catechists are also invited to accompany young people in their search for autonomy, even as new technologies allow

---

[543] *DC* 354.
[544] *DC* 355; cf. St John Paul II, *Fides et Ratio* (1998): 88.
[545] *DC* 356.
[546] *DC* 357.
[547] *DC* 358.
[548] *DC* 362.
[549] *DC* 359.
[550] *DC* 360.
[551] *DC* 361.
[552] *DC* 370.

for a more individualised approach to catechesis, since although catechesis might achieve more personalisation through technology, it should never be individualistic.[553] Finally, catechists are called to be an evangelising presence in the digital world.[554]

## Catechesis and Some Questions of Bioethics (paragraphs 373-378)

Because bioethics deals with questions regarding the beginning and end of life, as well as health and human experimentation, our Catholic faith has important contributions to make in this area.[555] While scientific fields such as genetics have improved the quality of life for many individuals, care must be taken that therapeutic intervention to support life does not cross the line to become manipulation of life, which would be contrary to the dignity of the human person and could lead to other morally problematic practices, such as eugenics.[556]

Also addressed in this portion of the *Directory* is the question of *gender theory*, which holds that gender identity is not biologically determined, but rather is a social construct. Here, the *Directory* acknowledges the complexity of the issues and the conflict that can arise within individuals who struggle with these issues while still affirming that God is creator and that human beings cannot create themselves.[557]

---

[553] *DC* 370, 372.
[554] *DC* 371.
[555] *DC* 373.
[556] *DC* 374-376.
[557] *DC* 377.

Regarding catechesis on bioethical issues, the *Directory* emphasises the need to promote moral formation that highlights the sanctity of human life as a gift from God that calls for respect for the dignity of the human person and of life as God has ordered it.[558] The following fundamental principles are offered:[559]

- God is the first and ultimate point of reference for life, from its conception until natural death;
- the person is always a unity of spirit and body;
- science is at the service of the person;
- life must be accepted no matter what its condition, because it has been redeemed by the paschal mystery of Jesus Christ.

## Catechesis and the Integrity of the Person (paragraphs 379-380)

The next two paragraphs of the *Directory* make a special appeal for catechists to take care to understand and promote the teachings of the Church regarding the dignity of the human person and the inviolability of life from conception to natural death.[560] In this way, catechesis contributes to the building of a culture of life.

## Catechesis and Environmental Engagement (paragraphs 381-384)

An additional challenge of modern times is posed by the unprecedented environmental threats we face – a particular concern of Pope Francis. In a series of paragraphs devoted to catechesis and environmental engagement, the *Directory for Catechesis* offers reflection on the role of the environment in Catholic spirituality and the responsibility of believers to care for the environment.

The *Directory* calls us to listen to "the cry of the earth" and the related "cry of the poor," who tend to be those most immediately affected by environmental crises, hearing in these dual cries the voice of God that calls us to promote an environmental spirituality among the faithful.[561] This requires, the *Directory* states, "fostering an attitude of respect toward all; teaching a correct conception of the environment and of human responsibility; educating people in a life that is virtuous, capable of adopting habits that are humble and sober, free from consumerism; bringing into focus the symbolic value of created realities, above all in the signs of the liturgy."[562] A commitment to care for the environment is, the *Directory* asserts, "an integral part of the Christian life."[563]

---

[558] *DC* 378.
[559] *DC* 378.
[560] *DC* 379-380.
[561] *DC* 382-383.
[562] *DC* 383.
[563] *DC* 384.

### Catechesis and the Option for the Poor (paragraphs 385-388)

Christ was drawn to the poorest of the poor, offering them blessing, empathy and care, and he called his followers to do the same.[564] As disciples of Jesus, we are called to follow his example by showing preferential love to those who have the least. A preferential option for the poor, then, is a well-established teaching throughout the history of the Church, stemming from our theological understanding rather than political, philosophical or social ideology.[565] In his teaching, Jesus proclaims that an encounter with the poor is a meeting with Christ himself: "whatever you did for one of these least brothers of mine, you did for me."[566] For this reason, we not only serve the poor, but are also blessed by them, since an encounter with the "least of these" is an encounter with the Son of God.[567]

Catechesis, the *Directory* instructs, should allow itself "to be challenged by poverty" and encourage "certain basic attitudes in the faithful: respect for the dignity of the person, support for his growth, promotion of the culture of fraternity, indignation over situations of misery and injustice."[568] We are also called to help others learn from the poor the virtue of poverty, not allowing ourselves to become too attached to material goods.

### Catechesis and Social Engagement (paragraphs 389-391)

We are created in the image of God who is a communion of Persons, and we have a responsibility to build a sense of communion with our families, and our larger communities. We are called to participation in society, solidarity with one another as one human family, and concern for the common good. For this reason, as Catholics, we work to identify and correct the causes of injustice in society.[569] Catechesis must help the faithful to understand the social teaching of the Church and to work to promote the common good in areas where injustice results from sinful social structures.[570] We are also called to support in a special way those whose work includes "social, cultural, media, economic, and political responsibilities."[571]

### Catechesis and the Work Environment (paragraphs 392-393)

This chapter closes with a discussion of catechesis and the work environment, pointing out that by his work as a carpenter Jesus bestowed the highest dignity on

---

[564] *DC* 386.
[565] *DC* 385.
[566] *DC* 386; *Matthew* 25:40 (NABRE).
[567] *DC* 387.
[568] *DC* 388.
[569] *DC* 389.
[570] *DC* 390.
[571] *DC* 391.

human work.[572] Catechesis affirms the truth that all adults who are able to do so have a right and responsibility to work. Everyone should have access to meaningful work, either inside or outside the home. Workers have a right to a just wage and fair working conditions, and Catholic workers have a responsibility to be witnesses of the Christian life in the workplace.[573]

## QUESTIONS FOR REFLECTION

1  What opportunities exist in your local community for engagement with non-Catholic Christians or communities of other religious faiths?
   • How might you use these opportunities in catechesis?

2  What are some ways to proclaim the social teaching of the Church in ways that are engaging and speak to the practical realities of the challenges presented by the culture around us?

---

[572] *DC* 392.
[573] *DC* 393.

# A Prayer for Catechists

LORD GOD,
You are present in the midst of the challenges
and needs in the world around us.
Help me to be a witness of your truth in society
and to teach others to do the same.
Fill us all with your Holy Spirit,
that we might work together with you as you build
   your kingdom.
We ask this in the name of Christ Jesus.
Amen.

# CHAPTER XI

# Catechesis at the Service of the Inculturation of the Faith

The Gospel is for every person, in every culture, and in every generation. The Catholic Church worldwide is rich in cultural diversity, and this is a sign of the fruitfulness of the Holy Spirit, reflected also in the ministry of catechesis and local catechisms.[574]

## NATURE AND GOAL OF INCULTURATION OF THE FAITH (paragraphs 395-400)

By becoming man and dwelling with us, Jesus Christ enculturated the word of God. As a Church, we are called to imitate this first inculturation through our own work in evangelisation. The *Directory* points out that this is an intentional and complex process: "Inculturation cannot be thought of as a mere adaptation to a culture. It is instead a profound, comprehensive, and progressive journey," with the ultimate aim of creating "a new synthesis" of the Gospel "with that particular culture."[575]

Inculturation of the Gospel message serves the work of evangelisation precisely because by situating the Gospel message in the context of a particular culture, we enter into the experience of persons. Inculturation is "aimed at the process of

---

[574] *DC* 394.
[575] *DC* 395.

internalisation of the experience of faith."[576] The *Directory* describes this work as particularly urgent, given that in many cases today "the cultural preconditions for the transmission of the Gospel, guaranteed in the past by family and society, have gone missing," leading to a critical need not merely to transmit the contents of the faith, but also to facilitate "the process of personal reception of the faith" – to form not only the head, but also the heart.[577]

Drawing upon earlier key documents in catechesis, the *Directory* offers the following "methodological guidelines" for inculturation of the faith:[578]

- getting to know deeply the culture of persons, activating relational dynamics marked by reciprocity that foster a new understanding of the Gospel;
- recognising that the Gospel possesses its own cultural dimension through which, over the course of the centuries, it has inserted itself into the different cultures;
- communicating the true conversion that the Gospel, as a force for transformation and regeneration, effects within cultures;
- making it understood that seeds of the Gospel are already present in cultures, although it transcends and is not exhausted in them;
- making sure that the new expression of the Gospel according to the culture being evangelised does not neglect the integrity of the contents of the faith, an important factor of ecclesial communion.

Quoting from the *GDC*, the *Directory* states that catechesis does not manipulate culture, but neither does it limit itself to "mere juxtaposition of the Gospel with culture in some 'decorative manner.'"[579] Instead, catechesis should engage with the very roots of culture in a dynamic and interactive process characterised by the following elements: "a listening in the culture of the people, to discern an echo (omen, invocation, sign) of the word of God; a discernment of what has an authentic Gospel value or is at least open to the Gospel; a purification of what bears the mark of sin (passions, structures of evil) or of human frailty; an influence on people through stimulating an attitude of radical conversion to God, of dialogue, and of patient interior maturation."[580]

The inculturation of the faith leads to an expression of the Gospel in the life of a community. It keeps the Gospel message alive and relevant to the people who live in that particular cultural context,[581] and leads to transmission of the faith that flows

---

576  *DC* 396.
577  *DC* 396.
578  *DC* 397.
579  *DC* 398; cf. *GDC* 204; *EN* 20.
580  *DC* 398; cf. *GDC* 204; *EN* 20.
581  *DC* 399.

not only from individuals, but from the culture as a whole.[582] In order to achieve these goals, catechists who are attempting to enculturate the Gospel message must look for the true, the good, and the beautiful in the culture, and connect these elements to the faith.

### LOCAL CATECHISMS (paragraphs 401-408)

Local catechisms are catechetical aids that both reflect and help to facilitate the inculturation of the Gospel. The local catechism strives to distill the faith in a way that is appropriate to a particular language and cultural context. They serve as a point of reference for catechesis in a particular diocese, region or nation.[583] The *Directory* discusses two primary features of catechisms: "they have an official character" (which makes them distinct from catechetical textbooks and other resources), and they are an organic and basic "summary of the faith", with a pedagogical focus that puts teachings into context.[584]

The *Catechism of the Catholic Church* is the point of reference for local catechisms, but the latter are not simply summaries of the former. Rather, local catechisms present the teachings articulated in the *Catechism* in the context of a specific cultural situation and for a particular audience.[585] Because the local Church is charged with

---

[582] *DC* 400.
[583] *DC* 401.
[584] *DC* 402.
[585] *DC* 403-404.

the inculturation of faith in a particular area, it is fitting for the local Church to develop local catechisms.[586]

The final paragraphs of this chapter discuss guidelines for obtaining approval from the Apostolic See for catechisms and other catechetical documents. This process is helpful, the *Directory* notes, because it allows the Apostolic See the ability to make suggestions as these documents are developed and because it allows the local Church a means with which to communicate with the Apostolic See about the context and catechetical needs in a particular area.[587] The *Directory* discusses the meaning of the term *prior approbation of the Apostolic See*, which is "a recognition of the fact that [a local catechism] is a text of the universal Church for a specific culture and situation."[588] Responsibility for approval of these documents rests with the Pontifical Council for the Promotion of the New Evangelisation, and is necessary for the following types of texts:

- national catechisms;
- national directories for catechesis or similar texts of like value;
- regional catechisms and directories;
- translations of the *Catechism of the Catholic Church* into the national languages;
- national scholastic texts in territories where the teaching of the Catholic religion has a catechetical value or where such texts are used in catechesis.[589]

## QUESTIONS FOR REFLECTION

1   What are the "seeds of faith" that exist in the culture in which you live?
   - How might you hold up what is good in the culture around you and use this as a foundation to proclaim the Gospel message?
2   Does your country or region have a local catechism?
   - If so, in what ways does your local catechism present the truths of the Catholic faith through the lens of your culture?

---

[586] *DC* 405.
[587] *DC* 407.
[588] *DC*; cf. *GDC* 285.
[589] *DC* 408.

# A Prayer for Catechists

GOD OF ALL PEOPLE,
You transcend the boundaries of country and culture.
Help us to enculturate your truth
in the context in which we live
and in other places where you might lead us.
Send us your Holy Spirit,
that we might find the means to connect your Word
with the everyday lives of those we serve.
We ask this in the name of Christ Jesus.
Amen.

# CHAPTER XII:

# The Organisms at the Service of Catechesis

## THE HOLY SEE (paragraphs 4093-410)

The Magisterium in general, and the Roman pontiff in particular, are visible signs of the unity of the Catholic Church. As successor of Peter, the pope is the "chief catechist" of the Catholic Church. His primary task, together with all of the bishops, is to proclaim and transmit the message of the Gospel; the Holy Father does this through his teachings (including his writings), his homilies, and his catecheses.[590] Within the present structure of the Holy See, on matters related to catechesis, the Holy Father typically acts through the Pontifical Council for the Promotion of the New Evangelisation, a dicastery of the Curia that was established by Pope Benedict in June of 2010 and was given oversight of catechesis in the Catholic Church in January of 2013.[591] The responsibilities of the Pontifical Council for the Promotion of the New Evangelisation with respect to catechesis include the following, as summarised in the *Directory for Catechesis*:[592]

- attends to the promotion of the religious formation of the faithful of every age and condition;

---

[590] *DC* 409.
[591] *DC* 410; cf. Benedict XVI, *Fides per Doctrinam* (16th January 2013).
[592] *DC* 410.

- has the faculty of issuing suitable norms so that catechesis may be carried out in an appropriate way according to the constant Tradition of the Church;

- has the task of ensuring that catechetical formation be carried out correctly in respect of methodologies and goals according to the guidelines of the Magisterium;

- grants the prescribed approval of the Apostolic See for catechisms and other writings relative to catechetical instruction;

- assists the catechetical offices within the episcopal conferences, follows their initiatives that concern religious formation and have an international character, co-ordinates their activities, and offers them any help that may be necessary.

## THE SYNODS OF BISHOPS OR COUNCILS OF THE HIERARCHY OF THE EASTERN CATHOLIC CHURCHES (paragraph 411)

Consistent with earlier content in the *Directory* on the importance of catechesis that embodies the unique cultural perspective and tradition of the Eastern Churches, The *Directory* affirms the responsibility of the hierarchy of the Eastern Churches to issue catechetical norms in the form of a catechetical directory, to plan catechetical initiatives, and to produce catechisms.[593] In this way, the Eastern Churches are able to make appropriate use of the gifts of their traditions while still teaching the faith in union with the universal Church.

## THE EPISCOPAL CONFERENCE (paragraphs 412-415)

Quoting Canon Law, this section of the *Directory* discusses the importance of the establishment of a *national catechetical office* by the local conference of bishops.[594] This office is responsible for assisting local bishops within the conference in a number of ways, including *"analysis of the situation* of catechesis in its territory,"* with the aim of formulating a national catechetical plan (which is co-ordinated with the plans of other national offices if more than one national office exists within the same episcopal conference) as well as preparing a national catechism.[595] The national catechetical office is also responsible for the formation of diocesan directors of catechesis, organisation of national catechetical events, and support of catechesis in under-resourced dioceses. Finally, the national catechetical office serves as a point of communication between the bishops of the episcopal conference and those responsible for preparing catechetical texts.[596]

---

[593] *DC* 411.
[594] *DC* 412.
[595] *DC* 413.
[596] *DC* 414.

## THE DIOCESE

The largest portion of this chapter on organisms at the service of catechesis is devoted to the diocese. This is fitting, since the bishop is responsible for catechesis in the local church, and resources provided by the diocese have the most direct influence on the parish, which is "the pre-eminent place for catechesis."[597] Because catechesis is "an activity so fundamental for the life of a particular Church," the *Directory* states, "every diocese is required to have its own catechetical office."[598] The *Directory* strongly recommends that the office be staffed by "an expert in catechesis" and that the work done by the office includes "priests, consecrated persons and the laity."[599]

The *Directory* outlines five key roles for the diocesan catechetical office. These bear strong similarities to the aforementioned roles of the national catechetical office:

- *Analysis of the situation*[600] – This includes study of both the socio-cultural factors at work in a particular diocese as well as *"analysis of the religious situation"*, including the current state of religious practice and knowledge of the faith. The *Directory* points out that it would be helpful to conduct this analysis in a structured, empirically-sound manner, rather than relying on anecdotal evidence, using "studies conducted by scientific institutions and by centres

---

[597] *CT* 67.
[598] *DC* 417.
[599] *DC* 417.
[600] *DC* 418-419.

of specialised research."[601] However, we are also warned against slipping into a "diagnostic overload"; rather, after a reasonable degree of analysis, we should use the data collected in the service of "evangelical discernment", with careful attention given to "the state of catechesis within the process of evangelisation."[602]

- *Co-ordination of catechesis*[603] – This role of the diocesan catechetical office involves collaboration with other pastoral ministries in order to make evangelisation efforts more effective. In particular, the *Directory* calls for "a close relationship with pastoral care for the family, young people, and vocations, as with pastoral care in schools and universities."[604]

- *The diocesan project of catechesis*[605] – Co-ordinated with, and complementary to, the general pastoral plan of the diocese, the diocesan programme of catechesis integrates the diverse catechetical programmes offered in the diocese. The *Directory* reiterates the directive of the 1997 *General Directory for Catechesis* that *adult catechesis* should be the organising principle for the diocesan plan, and that other catechetical activities, such as catechetical programmes for children and youth, should be organised around adult formation, rather than vice-versa. This is important for a variety of reasons. Firstly, children and adolescents must be catechised by well-formed adults, so without quality adult catechesis, quality children's catechesis is not possible. Secondly, children generally do not present themselves for catechesis. Adults will need to be well formed in order to take seriously their responsibility to raise their children in the faith, including ensuring that children are present in the Christian community. Finally, children are not formed in isolation. The seeds of discipleship sown with children and adolescents are most likely to bear fruit in the fertile soil of a family led by adults who are themselves intentional in their discipleship. The *Directory* recommends continuing to consider age level and developmental appropriateness with regard to organising the catechetical programme, but also calls catechetical leaders to consider other factors, such as "stages of growth in the faith" and the stage and station of life, or "existential situation" of participants.[606]

- *The practical programme*[607] – Described as the practical implementation of the diocesan programme of catechesis "for a specific situation and a limited

---

[601] *DC* 419.
[602] *DC* 419.
[603] *DC* 420-421.
[604] *DC* 420.
[605] *DC* 422-423.
[606] *DC* 423.
[607] *DC* 424.

time." The practical programme "identifies the contents, indicates the intermediate objectives – clear, step-by-step, measurable – provides activities and techniques, develops or indicates aids and materials and determines the schedules."[608] Also mentioned here is the importance of evaluation to facilitate improvements in the future.

- *Formation of catechists*[609] – Particular attention, the *Directory* states, should be given to the formation of catechists in the dimensions of catechist formation mentioned earlier in the *Directory*: being and being-with, knowledge, and *savoir-faire*, providing catechists with both "basic and ongoing formation", and providing catechetical leaders with "specialised formation".[610] Collaboration with other offices of the diocese as well as with the priests and lay people in the parish is also emphasised.

## QUESTIONS FOR REFLECTION

1   How attentive are you to the directives of, and the resources provided by, the Holy See, your local episcopal conference, and diocese?
    - How might their work offer you guidance and support in your ministry?
2   How might you contribute to the work of your diocesan office in the five key roles outlined in this chapter?

---

[608] *DC 424.*
[609] *DC 425.*
[610] *DC 425;* cf. *DC 136-150.*

# A Prayer for Catechists

LORD, YOU ARE THE GOOD SHEPHERD,
and you did not leave your flock with no one
    to watch over them.
Thank you for the gift of leaders in the Church.
We pray that you will bless them with wisdom
    as they guide your people.
Help us to be attentive to their leadership that
    we might be one in you.
We ask this in the name of Christ Jesus.
Amen.

# Conclusion

The *Directory* concludes, in paragraphs 426-427, with an affirmation of the Christocentricity of catechesis: "Communion with Jesus Christ, who died and rose again, who is living and always present, is the ultimate end of all ecclesial action and therefore of catechesis as well."[611]

On a related note, the *Directory* reiterates the importance of the *kerygma*: "The first profession of faith in the paschal mystery is the heart of the Church's faith."[612] Catechesis, here is expressed as an invitation to encounter Jesus, an "essential moment" in the process of evangelisation, leading "to the more conscious and intimate encounter with the Redeemer of humanity."[613]

Here also is discussed the role of Our Lady, who "educated Jesus...in the way of justice and obedience to the will of the Father" and "learned to follow the Son, becoming the first and most perfect of disciples."[614] In its closing lines, the *Directory* highlights Our Lady as "pedagogue of evangelisation and ecclesial model of the transmission of the faith."[615]

Indeed, may all who are called to the ministry of catechesis imitate Mary's openness to the will of God. May we allow Christ to grow within us, follow him as disciples, and lead others to him through our words and deeds.

---

[611] *DC* 426.
[612] *DC* 426.
[613] *DC* 427.
[614] *DC* 428.
[615] *DC* 428.